9/93

D0709491

Doing What the Day Brought

Mary Logan Rothschild   Pamela Claire Hronek

DOING WHAT THE DAY BROUGHT

An Oral History

of Arizona

Women

✦

The University of Arizona Press

TUCSON & LONDON

THE UNIVERSITY OF ARIZONA PRESS

Copyright © 1992
Arizona Board of Regents
All Rights Reserved

☉ This book is printed on acid-free, archival-quality paper.
Manufactured in the United States of America.

97 96 95 94 93 92   6 5 4 3 2 1

LIBRARY OF CONGRESS CATALOGING-IN-PUBLICATION DATA

Rothschild, Mary Aickin.
   Doing what the day brought : an oral history of Arizona women
/ Mary Logan Rothschild and Pamela Claire Hronek.
      p.   cm.
   Includes bibliographical references and index.
   ISBN 0-8165-1032-6. — ISBN 0-8165-1276-0 (pbk.)
      1. Women—Arizona—History—20th century.   2. Women—
Arizona—Biography.   3. Oral history.   I. Hronek, Pamela Claire,
1945–   .   II. Title.
HQ1438.A6R67   1992
305.4'09791'0904—dc20   91-20354
                                                                    CIP

British Library Cataloguing-in-Publication Data
A catalogue record for this book is available from the British Library.

To Our Parents
Orlean Longhurst Turner
and
Harvey and Ulla Rothschild
With Love

120
ROT

CONTENTS

✦

ACKNOWLEDGMENTS

✦

All of us who write oral history owe a great debt to the people who allow themselves to be interviewed so that we can get our stories, but none owe more than we do to the women we interviewed for this book, who were both gracious and enthusiastic about our project and lavished us with their time, their reminiscences, their reflections and, often, their food. Were it not for our desire to honor our parents, this book would be dedicated to all of the women who gave us their stories and helped us understand their role—and the roles of other women, too—in the building of Arizona.

In its earliest incarnation as "The Lives of Arizona Women: Public Issues and Private Conversations," this oral history project was funded by a generous and substantial grant from the Arizona Humanities Council. Arizona State University has also been generous in its support for this project: the provost funded the transcription of the interviews; the Women's Studies Program provided housing, staff, and supplies for the project; the University Word Processing Office typed several edited versions of the transcripts; and the dean of the College of Liberal Arts and Sciences twice funded Mary Rothschild through the Minigrant

Program to meet with Pamela Hronek to work on editing this book. The staffs of the Women's Studies Program and the History Department have been unstinting in their support and general help. Victoria Martinez and Jane Little of Women's Studies and Alice Valenzuela of History have literally worked on every draft of this project and have been cheerful in the face of adversity, rushed deadlines, and the authors' computer ignorance.

The original project had five staff members, some of whom were paid and some of whom were volunteers and all of whom worked hard. Mary Rothschild directed the project and Linda Salmon was the assistant director. Rose Diaz, Maria Hernandez, and Pamela Hronek all worked as interviewers, and Linda Salmon and Don Melichar did the photography.

Rose Diaz of the original project has continued to be interested and involved in western women's oral history and the oral history of ethnic communities. She has moved to New Mexico, where she is heading a major community oral history collecting project, and has been unfailing in her continuing support and enthusiasm for *Doing What the Day Brought*.

Three former students have done exceptional work in oral history and have been willing to share it with us. Valerie Matsumoto has allowed us to quote from her 1978 Honors Thesis, " 'Shikata Ga Nai': Japanese American Women in Central Arizona." Evelyn Cooper gave us the use of her interview with Charlie Mae Daniels. And Mary Melcher spent time explaining her understanding of the Civil Rights Movement in Phoenix. She also generously allowed us to use three of her unpublished papers, all of which are based on her solid work in oral history.

The *Scottsdale Daily Progress* graciously has allowed us to reproduce three pictures of women we interviewed taken by Suzanne Starr and published in an article entitled "Memories" on March 6, 1982.

The transcripts and many of the photographs from the Lives of Arizona Women Oral History Project are housed in the Arizona Collection of the Hayden Library at Arizona State University. Ed Oetting, who directs the Arizona Collection, and Chris

Marin, who heads the Chicano Studies Collection, have been helpful at every turn and speedy in filling requests.

Several friends have encouraged us at various stages of this project. Joanne O'Hare, our editor, has been both a strong support and a calming influence. Others have in equal parts inspired and prodded. Like us, they are all western women and all involved in the field of women's history. We want to give our warm thanks to Corky Bush of Idaho and Montana, Katherine Jensen of Wyoming, Sue Armitage and Nan Hughes of Washington, Rose Diaz and Joan Jensen of New Mexico, Valerie Matsumoto of California, and Pam Renner, Karen Anderson, Georganne Scheiner, and Mary Melcher of Arizona.

Finally, we want to say to Toby and Sasha Rothschild Aickin that their unique sense of humor has lightened the way and that they will soon have to find another topic to tease us about, since this book is now finished.

PREFACE

◆

This book is a story of women's experience in Arizona from the late nineteenth century to the present. Growing out of an oral history project funded by the Arizona Humanities Council and the Women's Studies Program at Arizona State University in 1981–82, and driven by the new field of women's history, this project was based on the work of Corky Bush in Idaho and Katherine Jensen in Wyoming, both of whom had organized women in their communities under the auspices of their humanities councils to conduct community-based women's oral history projects.[1]

All of us who worked on the Arizona project were excited about what was being done in other western states, and we were anxious to do a version of these other projects here in Arizona. We identified ourselves as women's historians, and we were western women as well. We knew that women had played a role in developing the West, and we believed that most women's lives had to date gone unnoticed in the traditional study of the West, dominated as it is by images of striving, aggressive Anglo men, who seem, in the main, unattached and alone against the wilderness.[2] All of us had a deep passion to redraw what we knew from our own lives was an inaccurate picture of western history, to unearth what women had done in Arizona, and to understand their role in developing this territory and state in the late nineteenth and early twentieth centuries.

We jumped at the chance for support from the Arizona Humanities Council and Arizona State University to conduct these oral histories, and we loved doing the project. This book comes from our belief that these women's stories deserve to be told to a larger audience yet, that Arizona women should begin to get their place in the sun from historians who have for years overlooked their considerable accomplishments.

WHAT WE DID ON THE PROJECT

The "Lives of Arizona Women Project," or "Lives" as we came to call it, had several bedrock premises: the first was that women were scandalously overlooked in the published histories of Arizona[3]; the second was that if women in general were overlooked, minority women were invisible; and the third was that we were interested in the lives of "ordinary" women, not the first doctor or professor or politician, but women who saw themselves as just like their neighbors and probably less worthy of interviewing. These premises directed our research and our interviewing to a large degree. For instance, we decided to conduct life course interviews, and we deliberately sought Black women, Hispanic women, and American Indian women, as well as Anglo women. Further, we chose women who represented the diversity of womankind in Arizona, crossing race, ethnic, religious, economic, and marital lines. While we did not necessarily feel that these women were prototypic of their respective groups, we strongly believed that making sure women of diverse backgrounds were included in the project would make the histories we gathered exemplary of the different kinds of lives women might have because of race, class, and ethnicity.

Women encounter some things solely because of their womanhood—menses, pregnancy, and gender-based job discrimination, for instance—but their race, class, and ethnicity may also cause them to experience those innately female things differently. For instance, Cecelia Sneezy, as an Apache Indian, proudly prepared for the onset of her menses, although in the end her grand-mother decided she could not afford to host a full Sunrise Dance to celebrate it. Contrast Sneezy's experience with almost all of the other women in the group who were totally unprepared for the onset of menses, terrified when it began, and who, in the case of Exie Zeiser, hid her menstruation for two years, never knowing what it was.

Race, class, and ethnicity also have a general effect on all people's lives, male and female. All minority men and women in Arizona experienced some, usually de facto, segregation in schools and public facilities. But some groups experienced discrimination differently and more powerfully; for example, only Japanese immigrants were forbidden by law to buy land, only Japanese Americans were interned in World War II, and only Black Arizonans were segregated in schools by law. We found ethnic and racial differences were particularly pronounced in the schooling and paid work experiences of the women we interviewed.

In deciding which individuals we would interview, we looked at census data from the period 1890 to 1930 and tried to replicate those proportions of, for example, ethnic minorities or married women in our interviews. We were also concerned to represent the dominant three economies in the state of mining, agriculture, and merchandising. To do that, we concentrated on interviewing women who lived in the rural Salt River Valley (around Phoenix) for ranching and farming, Phoenix for a merchant town economy, and Globe-Miami for a mining economy. Globe-Miami was also important because then, as now, the two mining towns were virtually completely segregated by ethnic group, with Globe being dominantly Anglo and Miami dominantly Hispanic. While we had an ideal about diversity and rough goals about whom to interview, we at no time believed we would have a scientific cross section of women in the state, and, in fact, we are perhaps underrepresented for Hispanic women and over-represented for Black women. Nevertheless, in gathering the oral histories, even with our imperfect representation, we have demonstrated the wide varieties in women's lives in the state.

To gather names of people to be interviewed, we put out a call for volunteers to local senior centers and civic groups, arranged to have stories done on the project in community newspapers and had public service announcements on the radio. We asked for women to nominate themselves or others who met the two main criteria of being over seventy years of age (in the end, we interviewed two women who were under seventy) and having lived all of their adult lives in Arizona (and preferably longer). We were stunned by the enormous response we received: more than two hundred women took the time to write or call us and then fill out a basic information sheet on their lives indicating their willingness to be interviewed. It was the single greatest sadness of the project that we only had the time and resources to interview about thirty women.

Mary Rothschild, who was then director of Women's Studies, headed the project and trained the interviewers, all of whom were students in American women's history at the graduate or advanced undergraduate level at Arizona State University. Interviewers for the project were Rose Diaz, Maria Hernandez, Pamela Hronek, and Linda Salmon, and they worked both on Arizona history and women's history to prepare the questions for the life course interviews they would conduct. Twenty-eight of the interviews were conducted in English and one in Spanish, and nearly every woman was interviewed multiple times. Additionally, we have been able to add to the original group of twenty-eight an interview by Evelyn Cooper of Charlie Mae Daniels conducted in 1981, an interview by Mary Rothschild of Cecelia Sneezy conducted in 1986, and interviews by Valerie Jean Matsumoto of Susie Sato, Mariyo Hikida, and Ayako Kanemura taken from her 1978 Arizona State University honors thesis, " 'Shikata Ga Nai': Japanese American Women in Central Arizona, 1910–1978." We have systematic basic data on the original twenty-eight as well as Cecelia Sneezy.

After the interviews were completed, a generous grant from the provost of Arizona State University allowed us to transcribe the taped interviews. These verbatim, unedited transcripts, which number more than fourteen hundred single-spaced pages, are in the Arizona Collection of the Hayden University Library at Arizona State University and form the body of the collection, "The Lives of Arizona Women: An Oral History Project," which is open to researchers.

In writing this book, we wanted to retain the sense and flavor of the women's own words, but we also wanted to write a more general, analytical history of Arizona women, using the oral histories we had gathered as the primary, but not only, data set. To achieve that goal, we decided to deviate from the norm in oral history books of simply presenting each woman's edited story, with a short introductory statement about the individual's life. Rather, we read all of the transcripts over and over again to get a sense of both typical and particular experiences in women's lives and then we chose examples to illustrate what it was like to be a woman in Arizona over the last century. To make sense of what we found and the bits and pieces of each woman's interview that we have put together, we have written a narrative to bind and explain the context. The women's stories are heavily edited, often drawn from different sections of an individual interview, and "cleaned up" sometimes to reflect the general language usage of the interview. If words are inserted that are not in the interview, however, standard scholarly notation marks the insertion. We hope that this model for publishing oral histories may prove useful to the developing field of twentieth-century western women's history.

Since we always had a double lens—to both see these women's lives and envision changing Arizona—we have attempted to follow a chronological frame within a topical approach. Chapter divisions are loosely chronological, but each discusses a general topic. "Coming to the Desert" deals with arriving in Arizona and what the land was like to new immigrants or young girls searching their memories. "Growing Up in Arizona" describes the childhood experiences of the women, their schooling, and coming of age. "Doing What the Day Brought" chronicles adult home life for the women, whether they were married or single, raising children or living alone. "Building Arizona's Communities" details the outstanding involvement of women in making

Arizona's social institutions, like schools, churches, hospitals, museums, and organizations. "Working for Pay in a Man's World" shows the variety of jobs women held in Arizona and the importance their work had for the developing economy. And, finally, "Reflecting on Change" sums up the women's thoughts about their lives and the extraordinary development they have witnessed in the state of Arizona.

INTRODUCTION: FRAMING ARIZONA WOMEN'S HISTORY

✦

Few of us can imagine how recent the "Old West" is in Arizona. We have pictures in our minds, in which brave Anglo men wore guns and rode horseback, and lonely Anglo women did their best to civilize desolate homesteads. Indians lived in tepees, and towns were rough, with unpaved streets lined with hitching posts along the side. The truth is that all of these idealized western pictures, which most of us place in the nineteenth century and imbibed from movies, Zane Grey novels, and television, could be seen in Arizona in the span of a twentieth-century lifetime.

The pioneer experience in Arizona is a recent one. The women we interviewed gathered dead saguaro cactus ribs to make outdoor fires to boil the water for their laundry, searched for desert herbs to make home medicines, and had routine run-ins with desert "critters"—scorpions, rattlesnakes, coyotes, and, in one memorable instance in the mountains, a bear. One woman we interviewed gave birth to her first child in her tepee on a dirt floor in the 1930s. Several remember the joy of the occasional trip to town, where, if they were very lucky, they might have a bowl of soup in a restaurant before the long ride home in their buggy. Many struggled with the mud in downtown Phoenix's unpaved

streets during the rainy season, and commuting students routinely rode their horses to college, hitching them to posts outside
Old Main at Tempe Normal School well into the teens.

For those who know Phoenix today, with its population of
roughly two million, pollution, cars, noise, and bustle, try to
imagine what it was like to know that every spring you would
gather your friends and family together, hitch up your horse to
your buggy, and drive a few miles to picnic in a desert carpeted
with wildflowers. Or imagine seeing every mountain on the ho-
rizon crystal clear every day, unless there was a dust storm.

All of the women we interviewed experienced this Arizona in
their lifetimes. Their stories are really an amalgam of the transformation wrought by population, development, technology,
and the evolution of women's roles in the "New West." These
women's stories are an attempt to understand the changing lives
and changing state of women in Arizona.

AN OVERVIEW OF WOMEN IN THE WEST

In a general sense, women fared better in the West than they did
in other sections of the United States. They had a higher economic position, they were more likely to be employed in professional occupations, and they had a higher legal status than
women in other regions. Scholars are divided on the reasons for
this, but some likely causes are that women were numerically
scarce in the West and that the uneven sex ratio, which often
changed radically in a very few years, made men more appreciative of women and more amenable to accepting women in nontraditional positions. There is also the belief that the frontier was
inherently more democratic than more settled areas and that this
democratic tendency allowed women's issues to be considered
more seriously, and acted upon more easily, in the West. Some
speculate that those women and men who had the courage and
desire to change their lives drastically by moving West were also
more likely to be receptive to change in women's status than
those who stayed in more settled regions. Lastly, especially in the
territories that had a Spanish legacy, such as Arizona, the Spanish
concept of "community property" had a profound legal effect on

all married women, for it gave them equal access to all the accumulated real and movable property of the marital community, as well as equal status in guardianship of their children. This liberated women from the English common law tradition of "femme couverte" that held married women to be "dead-in-the-law," and which forbade them to sue or be sued, to have guardianship of their children, to own property, to retain either their own or their husband's wages, or to make contracts.

The roles women played in changing the West are also under considerable scholarly debate.[1] Julie Roy Jeffrey in *Frontier Women* found that the women she studied were civilizers who worked hard to recreate the same standard of behavior and decorum they had in their region of origin.[2] Jeffrey's women's attempts to recreate traditional visions of women's piety, purity, passiveness, and domesticity, what Barbara Welter[3] and other historians have called "true womanhood," are at odds with what Sandra Myres found in her work *Westering Women*.[4] Myres's women are adventurous and ready to break out of the old patterns, adapting relatively easily to their new western homes. Somewhere between these two visions, Ruth Moynihan, Susan Armitage, and Christiane Fischer Dichamp have found the women whose accounts of western living they have edited in *So Much to Be Done* "exhibit both tendencies."[5] On the issue of whether or not women and men experienced westward migration similarly—were women dragged reluctantly or did they come willingly—the first serious work has been done on the earliest period by John Mack Faragher in his *Women and Men on the Overland Trail* and Lillian Schlissel in her *Women's Diaries of the Westward Journey*.[6] They found that women and men experienced the move West differently, sometimes both simultaneously dreading and anticipating the move.

The women whose oral histories we collected certainly represented all of these traits. All were civilizers in one degree or another, though few were as clear as Violet Irving's grandmother who, no matter what she was doing, at four o'clock in the afternoon donned a new apron and had a formal tea with her husband, who stopped work on the ranch regardless of what he was doing to join her, and any neighbors who might have dropped by, for this daily ritual. And all were adventurers, adapting, some with more grace and ease than others, to the new desert life. On migration, we found that women often had a harder time than men, at least sometimes because of their child-bearing and child rearing responsibilities. We also found there were differences in when the women migrated: generally women who came by train in the twentieth century had an easier time than women who came earlier, perhaps with less choice and certainly with more hardship, by wagon. But we also interviewed adventurous women who came on their own as young adults, entranced by the desert and in search of new opportunities. Like the women in *So Much to Be Done*, the women we interviewed represented all of the major schools in western history so far.

SETTLEMENT IN ARIZONA

Before Arizona had independent territorial status, Congress had already established Arizona's first American Indian reservation in 1859 for the Pima and Maricopa Indians. Also living in Arizona at that time were the Navajo, Hopi, Havasupai, Mohave, Yavapai, Papago, Yuma, Walapai, and Apache. Although Mexican and Anglo settlement has transformed the population of Arizona since 1859, American Indians have remained a significant part of the territorial and state population. In 1980, Arizona had the second largest Indian population of any state with 128,664 Indians living within its borders, surpassed only by California.[7]

Early figures for settlement in Arizona are difficult to assess precisely because census takers often did not count all people. Generally, in the early censuses, though not always, census takers systematically counted only white settlers, and then, in the case of women, often only women of "good repute." While for every census there are figures for minorities, it is clear from household studies and reservation figures that Mexican Americans, African Americans, and American Indians were often seriously undercounted and rarely systematically surveyed. Nevertheless, it is possible to say that Anglo and Mexican settlement patterns in Arizona reflected the same uneven sex ratios as the rest of the West from the beginning. In the 1870 census, which seems to be accurate for white settlers and was completed less than seven years after territorial status was granted, the white population of Arizona was 9,581, with 6,834 men and 2,747 women, which is a ratio of 248.8 males to every 100 females, while the reported total population, which is less reliable, was 9,658—6,887 men and 2,771 women. During the next decade the population of the territory grew enormously to over 35,160 whites, 24,556 of whom were men and 10,604 of whom were women, yet the sex ratio of 231.6 men to every 100 women represented little change. The total population was counted as 40,440—28,202 men and 12,238 women. By 1890, the gap between white men and women settlers was closing, with 33,405 men and 22,175 women for a sex ratio of 150.6 to every 100 women. Census takers put the total population for the territory at 88,243—50,743 men and 37,500 women, for a sex ratio of 135.3 men to every 100 women. This 1890 ratio remained relatively stable until 1920, when the total white population was 291,449, with 159,345 men and 132,104 women for a ratio of 120.6 men to 100 women. The pattern for the total population, put at 334,162, with 183,602 men and 150,560 women, remained the same.[8]

Population centers in Arizona have changed profoundly in the century from 1870 to 1970. In 1870 Tucson was by far the largest town with a population of 3,224. The next largest town was Yuma, known then as Arizona City, at 1,142. Prescott, the territorial capitol, was 676, and Adamsville and La Paz, both ghost towns by 1910, outdistanced Phoenix whose population was 246. By 1890, there was a pattern of steady growth, with several substantial new mining towns, like Florence, Tombstone, and Nogales, all of which had populations over one thousand. Tucson remained the largest city at 5,150, but Phoenix had grown tremendously to 3,152. By 1910 the mining town population dominated growth in the territory, with Bisbee, Clifton, Douglas, Globe, and Prescott all ranging from approximately 5,000 to 10,000 residents. While Tucson remained the largest town at 13,193, Phoenix had grown to 11,134. By 1920, Phoenix overtook Tucson as the primary population center in the state with 29,053 to Tucson's 20,292, and mining towns remained relatively stable or began to decline. Both Phoenix and Tucson became established as the dominant urban areas in Arizona and by 1970 had populations of 581,562 and 262,933, respectively. Maricopa County's 1970 population was 969,425, while Pima County's was 351,667. No other county in the state was larger than 68,000.[9]

In the late nineteenth and early twentieth centuries, settlers tended to be either ranchers and farmers or miners. Mining and agriculture dominated Arizona's economy until well into the twentieth century when the extraordinary sunbelt migration, with tourism, manufacture, and urban development, changed the entire state into the urban Arizona of today.[10]

WOMEN IN ARIZONA TERRITORY AND EARLY STATEHOOD

For the first twenty years after territorial status was granted in 1863, politics in Arizona was concerned primarily with law and order issues and was dominated by the Democratic Party. Politicians sought to present a view of a stable, promising frontier in order to attract more population and investment. Developing Arizona communities was necessary for that agenda to succeed. While only white men were represented politically, women were active in community building, which they saw as political work. Women such as Caroline Cedarholm and Lizzie Garrison worked as teachers, physicians, and missionaries in Prescott in 1870, organizing temperance meetings and trying to clean up Prescott's famous "Whiskey Row" with a special ministry to local prostitutes.[11] Also involved in community work, Sallie Davis Hayden was the postmistress of Hayden's Ferry (later renamed Tempe) from 1876 to 1878. She became a member of the local school board and worked hard to upgrade education in the area. She opened a library in her home, which also served as a boarding house for teachers, professors, and visitors to Tempe. Keenly interested in politics, Sallie Hayden was an early leader in the territorial women's suffrage movement and often campaigned effectively for male politicians.[12]

Women became more directly involved in Arizona politics through the fight over the suffrage amendment. Early in 1881, Representative Murat Masterson of Prescott introduced an act in the Territorial Legislative Assembly entitled "To Extend the Right of Suffrage to Women." Masterson's proposition was defeated as were similar propositions in 1883 and 1885. By the time the issue of women's suffrage was again raised at the first Arizona Constitutional Convention in 1891, women of the Territory had formed their own suffrage associations to support the effort, led by temperance women such as Josephine Hughes of Tucson, Frances Munds of Prescott, and Mormon women such as Mary J. R. West and Mabel Ann Morse Hakes, both presidents of their local Relief Societies.[13]

During the first Constitutional Convention in 1891, women's suffrage was one of several Populist issues considered; others included were initiative, recall, referendum, and free silver. Members of the convention were divided between progressives, who were most concerned with the Populist issue of inflating money, and conservatives, who opposed almost all of the Populist planks. Caught between the two factions, women's suffrage did not garner enough votes to be included in the proposed constitution. Ultimately, however, the United States Congress turned down the proposed constitution and statehood for Arizona because of the decidedly Populist cast of the document. Arizona was not allowed to petition again for statehood until 1910.[14]

Although women had lost that round, the fight for suffrage did not end with the first Constitutional Convention. In 1903, after considerable lobbying by pro-suffrage forces, the Territorial Legislature finally passed a women's suffrage bill. Unfortunately for its supporters, Territorial Governor Alexander Brodie vetoed the bill, allegedly on constitutional grounds. This ended legislative action on suffrage until the second Constitutional Convention in 1910, although women's suffrage supporters presented their demands for suffrage to every Territorial Legislature and vowed to remember who had supported them when they finally received the vote.

In 1910, when Arizona was again allowed to hold a Constitutional Convention, the National American Women's Suffrage Association sent organizers and money into the state in hopes of having women's suffrage written into the proposed constitution.

Then, by themselves, Arizona women formed a new Arizona Equal Suffrage Association. Despite all their lobbying, women's suffrage was not part of the original constitution, which was ultimately accepted by Congress in 1911.[15]

Arizona women's suffrage supporters began an initiative campaign for women's suffrage once Arizona achieved statehood under the new constitution, which included the people's power to make laws by initiative. On July 5, 1912, the first possible day, supporters filed enough petitions to place women's suffrage on the ballot. Both the Democratic and Republican parties supported the initiative. The Democrats' support was the important endorsement, however, because of the extraordinary dominance of the Democratic Party in the state. Women's suffrage passed overwhelmingly in November of 1912, carrying every county in the new state.[16]

With the passage of the women's suffrage initiative, Arizona became one of the nine states in the nation to have full women's suffrage. Eight of the nine were in the West: Wyoming, Colorado, Utah, Idaho, Washington, California, Oregon, and Arizona, with Kansas also joining the suffrage ranks in 1912. Early women's suffrage was a western phenomenon and demonstrated that western men were more receptive to equal rights for women than men in other regions. Nevertheless, as is clearly reflected in the Arizona experience, at no time and in no place did women's suffrage come without a struggle.[17]

Immediately upon winning the vote, Arizona women began working in politics as politicians and volunteers. Attaining suffrage meant a great deal to women throughout the state and established them in a tradition of community and political involvement.[18]

From early territorial days, then, women worked to settle Arizona, to promote community betterment, and to extend their political power to attain the right of suffrage. These issues mobilized hundreds of Arizona women, though we know the names of only the relatively famous, like Sallie Davis Hayden and Frances Munds.

The histories in this book, in the main, represent a later stage in Arizona history, though certainly some of the women were alive when the territorial and statehood fight over suffrage began, and many supported suffrage, like Edna Brazill, who wrote her senior high school essay in Illinois on "The Value of Woman's Suffrage" and moved to Arizona on her own after her graduation from college.

The legacy of women's activism and agency that has been traced here blossomed into full flower as the twentieth century progressed. The stories that follow will begin to open up to public view the wide range of women's activities in Arizona, not just "famous" women's work, but the everyday work that "ordinary" women did to create today's Arizona.

The women we interviewed share some general characteristics. Twenty-two are Anglos, while two are American Indians, two are Hispanics, and three are Black. About a third were born in the decade of the 1890s and about forty percent were born in the first decade of the new century. When we interviewed them in 1981, the women ranged in age from 91 to 67 years. Including Cecelia Sneezy, who was born in 1921 and not interviewed until 1986 when she was 65, only three were born after Arizona attained statehood. Overwhelmingly, the women we interviewed were westerners. Thirteen were actually born in Arizona and nine more were born in the nearby states of Colorado, New Mexico, Oklahoma, Texas, and Chihuahua, Mexico. One was born in Europe, one in the Deep South, one in the East, and four in the Midwest.

Assessing social class is not easy, because many people assume they are middle-class, whether they are really richer or poorer than that. Further, definitions depending on property ownership may not mean the same thing when the property owned is a substantial house in Bisbee or a hardscrabble homestead in the Salt River Valley. Also, especially in the fluid frontier, families' and individuals' fortunes changed over time, sometimes very quickly, and so even someone raised generally in comfortable surroundings may have had a lean time or two. Nevertheless, a *very* rough estimate holds that twenty of the women were from middle-class families, while six were from working-class families and three from very poor families. As adults, there seemed to be some class mobility, with twenty-six women judged to be middle-class and three working-class. These assessments are estimates only, and what seems like middle-class life in 1900 might well be adjudged close to poverty in 1990.

Like class, family occupation varied over the childhoods of the women we interviewed, but we assessed occupation on the dominant parental jobs during the women's childhoods. Thirteen grew up in farming and ranching households and only two in mining homes. Nine women had parents who were merchants or business people, while three had fathers who were laborers. Only one had a father in government service. During their own adulthoods, their dominant household occupations changed somewhat. Reflecting the shifts in Arizona's economy, only five lived as farmers or ranchers, and none were in mining families in the mid-twentieth century. While there were still nine in merchant-business families, though not exactly the same nine, the growth came in the professional class, with five women living in households supported by male professionals, like lawyers or doctors, and six women supporting themselves and their households by teaching. The number of laborer and government worker households remained the same.

Although it is hard to correlate the education of the women we interviewed to the census data for education in Arizona, it is clear that they were relatively highly educated for their time. Education data from 1900 to 1930 is difficult to analyze, because age grading was not standardized, as it generally is today, and the data were not gathered by class level, but rather by age, which makes it difficult to know what kind of school students were attending. Several of the women we interviewed attended normal school to become teachers by the time they were fourteen, and it was common for rural school teachers in 1900 to be merely a few years older than their students and never to have attended post–high school classes. Further, although the data are divided by race, the definitions varied, and the three categories were white, Negro, and "Other races," which sometimes, but not always, included Mexicans, American Indians, and Asians. Categories were not consistent, and even "whites" were divided into native born and foreign born. Often foreign-born Hispanics were considered foreign-born whites, while native-born Hispanics were considered "Other races." For these reasons, we are using total numbers only. Further, because of the variations in age of starting school, the census categories of ages "10 to 14" and "15 to 20" seem to be the most likely to be useful. In 1910, 77 percent of Arizona girls between the ages of 10 and 14 were attending school, while by 1920, attendance had risen to 81.9 percent. In 1920, 34.1 percent of young women 15 to 20 were attending some form of school, and by 1930 that number had risen to 42.5 percent.[19] By contrast, the women we interviewed all attended elementary school, though one only went through the primary grades, and fully 93 percent attended high school. Sixty-two percent took post–high school training and 52 percent of those attended college or normal school, graduating with either a baccalaureate degree or a teaching certificate. Finally, four of these women, all teachers, took post-baccalaureate training for professional advancement.

Like most women of the time, nearly all of the women married at least once: only three remained single their entire lives. But five of the women divorced, while eight of the women were either divorced or widowed before they were 40. By the time we interviewed them, twenty-one of the twenty-six women who married had been widowed at least once, while several had been widowed or divorced more than once and six had remarried at least once. Four of the women had married by age 18 and a total of eighteen were married by age 25. By contrast, five of the women contracted their first marriage after the age of 30, with one woman marrying for the first time at age 52.

Childbearing and rearing was a common bond, and twenty-one of the married women had children. While five married women remained childless, none of these married before the age of 32 and four after the age of 36, with two divorcing less than two years after their marriages. None of the single women had children, though one helped support nieces and nephews.

Although group statistics give a picture of the overall contours of the lives of the women we interviewed, individual sketches provide a context for their stories. The following introductions to the twenty-nine women we interviewed are intended simply to give a framework to understand the women's stories and are presented in a chronological order, beginning with the oldest woman we interviewed, Clara Kimball, and continuing to the youngest, Cecelia Sneezy.

Exemplary of early Mormon settlers in Arizona, Clara Curtis was born in 1890 on a ranch in St. David and was the only woman we interviewed who grew up in a polygamous family. A fine pianist, she studied music at the University of Southern California to become a teacher and married her husband, Gordon Kimball, shortly after he returned from his mission as required by the Mormon church in 1910. Together they had four children. She was widowed in 1975.

Nora Neavitt McKinney was born in Texas in 1891 and moved to Arizona in 1912 as a young married woman with one child. She taught school, after the birth of her second child, in rural York, Arizona, from 1914 to 1916. Her husband was a cowboy and rancher, and she always commercially farmed some acreage in fruits and flowers. Following her husband's death in 1952, she supported herself by doing a series of varied jobs, including staffing in the state legislature, running a motel, and teaching leather crafting.

Elsie Rogers's parents moved to Arizona from New Mexico in 1895 when she was a baby. She married her first husband in 1914 and divorced him after their only child, who was very ill his entire life, had reached adulthood. She later married Dan Dunn in 1937 and had her second child at the age of 42. She lived all over the state on farms and ranches. As an adult, she was a homemaker and also was often employed. Among her many paid jobs, she worked in an aircraft factory during World War II and later in a hospital in housekeeping. She was widowed at age 60.

Madge Johnson was also born in 1895 and was the only woman we interviewed who came from the Deep South. Madge married in 1917, had her first child in 1918, and moved to Arizona the next year when her marriage failed. Shortly after she moved to

Phoenix, she married Clarence Copeland and had two more children. Widowed in 1929, she opened the first beauty parlor for Black women in Phoenix and went on to become the first Black appointed Deputy County Recorder in Arizona. Madge was extremely active in the fight for desegregation in Arizona.

Edna Porch was the third woman we interviewed who was born in 1895. She moved to Arizona as a young woman from Illinois after college in 1918 and taught until she married her husband, John Brazill, in 1919. Edna had one child and worked with her husband in the mortuary they owned in Glendale. Very active in community concerns, Edna was widowed at the age of 79.

Born in Snowflake, Arizona, in 1896, Irma Hanson grew up in a Mormon ranching community where her family helped build the church and school. She married Karl West in 1915 and had seven children. She worked with her husband on their ranch and held every post open to women in her Mormon Church.

Lupe Nunez was born in Chihuahua, Mexico, in 1897. She married Enrique Hernandez in 1915 and had four children, two of whom died, before they moved to Arizona in the middle of the Madero Revolution. Just before she left Mexico, Lupe lost her premature newborn daughter, at least partially, she believes, as a result of having been taken by soldiers out in the desert without water and food. After moving to Miami, Arizona, where her husband worked in the mines, Lupe had three more children. Widowed at age 33, Lupe had to work night and day as a house cleaner and laundress to support herself, her five children and the four brothers and sisters-in-law she raised when her mother-in-law died, and the two nieces she raised when her brother-in-law's wife died. Altogether Lupe raised eleven children and also accumulated enough, with her own and her children's work, to buy and rebuild a house of her own.

Winona Montgomery was born in 1898 in Nebraska and moved to Arizona in 1919 after college. Remaining happily single all her life, Winona taught school around the state, but primarily in Phoenix, where she built a house and was extremely active in community affairs and teachers' organizations.

Born on a ranch in Tempe, Arizona, in 1898, Irene Redden

lived in Tempe all her life and was an active member of the community. She married Gene Bishop in 1919, after she completed a course at Tempe Normal School. Irene had one daughter and was primarily a homemaker until she opened a guest ranch as part of their family working ranch in 1930. When World War II made staffing too difficult, she closed the guest ranch.

Anne Pace was also born in Arizona in 1898, growing up in Thatcher, a Mormon community. After receiving a degree at the University of Arizona, she married Julius Bush, a mining engineer, in 1924, and lived most of her adult life in Miami. She had two children and was a social worker for the state of Arizona for twenty-three years. Anne was widowed in 1968.

Brenda Weisburg was born in Russia at the turn of the century and immigrated to the United States in 1904, moving to Phoenix in 1915, where she immediately looked up members of the Jewish community. In 1937 she left for Hollywood where she was a successful screen writer. She returned to Phoenix in 1951. She married Morris Meckler in 1952 and was widowed in 1979. Brenda continues to write professionally for magazines and was formerly involved in the theater community in Phoenix.

Born in 1901 in Bull Creek, Oklahoma, Exie Ridgeway moved to Arizona at the age of 17. She married Nicholas Zieser, a bricklayer, in 1928, and had three children. Because her husband went blind and was unable to work, Exie supported the family by doing office work and bookkeeping while her husband took care of the children. Exie was widowed at the age of 52, when her youngest child was 8.

Marjorie Harris was born and raised in New York City. In 1924 she moved to Arizona at the age of 23 because she married Kaufman Mandell, a merchant in Florence and Casa Grande. She helped her husband in his business and had one child in 1926. She maintained her Jewish traditions even in small-town Arizona and was widowed in 1974.

Violet Milliken was also born in 1901 in Walker, Arizona. She married for the first time in 1918. Within weeks of her first child's premature birth and while the baby was still in an incubator, her young soldier husband died of the Spanish flu, leaving her a widow. She supported her family as a payroll accountant for the Santa Fe Railroad, later marrying John Warren in 1923. She had her second child in 1925 and was again widowed in 1938, after which she took over her husband's general store in Skull Valley. She married Harry Irving in 1948 and was widowed again in 1962. She continued working in the store and as postmistress until she was forced to retire in 1971.

Born in 1902 in Illinois, Mary Carter moved with her family to Tempe in 1914, where she lived the rest of her life. After marrying John Moeur in 1921, while he was in medical school at the University of Illinois, she had a son in 1923. Her husband was one of the town doctors and they owned a ranch, but he became an invalid early, and she was widowed at age 32. She raised her son and her orphaned niece by herself and took care of her invalid mother, working at a variety of jobs, including ranching, running the cotton office, and being a Congressional aide part-time in Washington, D.C. With Irene Bishop, she was a founder of the Tempe Historical Museum.

Edna Phelps was born in St. Louis in 1905 and moved with her family to homestead a farm in Phoenix in 1914. She attended business school and then Phoenix College, where she won a scholarship to the University of Southern California. Upon graduation, she taught for many years, until she married at the age of 32 and was not allowed to continue teaching. She divorced her husband, who had courted her for ten years, after twenty months and never remarried. Edna taught and did office work to support herself and was active in politics and community affairs.

Benita Yeager was born in the Adams Hotel, Phoenix's best, in 1906, because her parents had a large sheep ranch north of Prescott, far away from medical care. Benita grew up in Glendale on a ranch and graduated from the University of Arizona as a teacher. She married Richard Fennemore, a young lawyer, in 1932, and had two children. She was a homemaker and active volunteer in Phoenix cultural activities. Benita was widowed in 1969.

Born in Globe, Arizona, in 1907, Elsie Gates lived there all her life. She graduated from Arizona State Teachers College and taught before her first marriage when she was 24. After having two children, she divorced her first husband in 1937 and taught school to support her family. She later married Max McAlister in 1938 and had two more children. She was a substitute teacher for most of her life and was widowed at the age of 71.

Loretto Coles was also born in an Arizona mining town in 1907. A native of Bisbee where her father was a banker and store owner, she attended a Catholic girls' school in Hollywood, California, and later Phoenix College and the University of Arizona. After college, she moved to Phoenix to work in, and ultimately manage, her father's home furnishing store. Remaining single all of her life, Loretto took care of her invalid father until he died and also took primary financial responsibility for her brother's four children after his death.

Born in Colorado in 1907, Jane Wilson moved to Arizona with her family when she was five. After high school, she became a social worker for many years and later worked in her parent's store in Globe. She married A. Herbert Drees in 1944 at the age of 37. He was an accountant and she continued her work at the family store, ultimately buying it with her brother-in-law in 1965. Jane was extremely involved in Republican Party politics and community work. She was widowed in 1975.

Elfleda Fern Foltz was born on a ranch in Phoenix in 1908 and lived all her life in the Salt River Valley. Known as Fern, she attended Arizona State Teachers College and became a teacher at Madison School. In 1931 Fern married Raymond Johnson, a farmer in Peoria, where she lived, worked on the farm, and substitute taught for over thirty years. Fern had three children and was very active in local school and church work.

Mary Elizabeth Smith, known as "Mae," was born in Carlsbad, New Mexico, in 1909 and moved to Arizona with her family when she was five. They lived in mining towns all over the state, where her father worked as a miner and a hauler of ore. When she finished high school in 1927, Mae married Harley Wills, and they had one son in 1929. Mae traveled with her husband in his work as a highway maintenance man. Later, she helped him in several family businesses, including running a service station and a general store. She was widowed in 1970 at the age of 61.

Tillie Claire Mandelowitz was born in Albuquerque in 1909 and moved with her family to Nogales in 1916. She took a degree in elementary education at Arizona State Teachers College and later a secondary education degree at the University of Arizona, and worked as a teacher for forty-four years. She married when she was 36 years old but divorced her husband in less than a year. She later married Leon Garten in 1963, when she was 54. Tillie is active with the Phoenix Artists' Guild and in the Jewish community.

Lupe Lopez, nicknamed "Ruby," was born in Globe, Arizona, in 1910. Her father died when she was a teenager and her mother took over the family hardware store, with the help of her eleven children, including Ruby. After high school, Ruby went to Arizona State Teachers College to be a teacher, but she married Rafael Carlos Estrada, a young teacher, in 1932. Ruby had two children by 1934 when her husband decided to go to law school at the University of Arizona. He continued teaching while he was in law school and they ultimately had four children. Returning to Phoenix after her husband finished his degree, Ruby raised her children and helped her husband in his law office. Ruby was widowed in 1979 at the age of 69.

Irene McClellan was born in Oklahoma City in 1911 and moved with her family to Laveen, Arizona, when she was nine years old. As a young Black girl, she experienced school segregation in the Phoenix area through high school. When she went to college at Arizona State Teachers College, however, classes were integrated. When she graduated, Irene began teaching at Booker T. Washington Elementary School in Phoenix and then taught forty years at Dunbar School. Irene married Newman King in 1947 when she was 36 years old. She is active in the Phoenix Black community, the YWCA, and teachers' organizations.

Elizabeth Jessop was born in Morenci, Arizona, in 1911 and has lived nearly all of her life in the state. After high school, she attended business school and worked in assorted clerical office and sales jobs as an adult. Elizabeth married Oscar Hovde in 1934, and they lived on their farm in the Salt River Valley. She had two children and now lives with her husband in Leisure World in Mesa.

Born in Texas in 1912, Veora Johnson came to Mesa, Arizona, at the behest of the principal of her Normal School, to teach in the new Mesa school. Setting out on her own as a young Black woman only sixteen years old, Veora remained in the Mesa school district throughout her working life, attaining various administrative positions, including principal and curriculum consultant. She did a substantial amount of post-graduate work and remained single all of her life.

Sallie Simms was born in Parker, Arizona, in 1914, on the Mohave Indian Reservation. Her father was Mohave and her mother was half Mohave and half Quechan. They farmed on the reservation and she began government boarding school near La Mesa at age 6. As a teenager, after a bout with tuberculosis, which killed two of her siblings, she attended boarding school in Tucson and later the University of Arizona, where she studied to be a teacher. In 1936, Sallie married Roe Blaine Lewis, who was half Pima and half Papago Indian. Lewis was a teacher who became a Presbyterian minister fifteen years after they were married. They had three children, and Sallie worked as a homemaker and minister's wife, doing an extraordinary amount of women-oriented church work.

Cecelia Valasquez was born in White River, Arizona, on the Apache Reservation in 1921. From the age of 5, she lived with her grandmother and her brothers and sisters in a tepee on the reservation. She attended a mission day school until she became ill with tuberculosis at the age of 14 and had to drop out. In 1937, Cecelia's grandmother arranged a traditional marriage for her, and Cecelia met her husband at her wedding. She had her first daughter a year later when she was 17 in her grandmother's tepee with a dirt floor. Her grandmother, a midwife, delivered the baby. Cecelia divorced her first husband after less than two years and in 1941 married Fred Sneezy, who was a tribal policeman.

They had seven children. Cecelia was a homemaker and worked in Democratic Party politics in her tribe. Later in her life, she worked at Globe High School in an Apache heritage program to teach Apache language, history, and customs to high school students. Cecelia was widowed in 1981.

These women's stories begin with their response to the desert. For some, it was their home from birth; for others it was the end of the long road of migration. Their reactions to the desert were as varied as their personalities—some cursed a terrain they found harsh and bleak, while others saw beauty immediately. Adapting to the desert, raising their families, and building their communities was the heart of their lives. Through their words, we hope you will see how, as Fern Johnson said, Arizona women "did what the day brought" and fashioned much of what Arizonans now hold dear about their state.

Doing What the Day Brought

COMING TO THE DESERT

✦

*The desert is something that at first you fear, but then
you learn to love it.*   Marjorie Mandel

Regardless of the mode of transportation, whether one came by
wagon or by train, the journey to Arizona was difficult. Women
who came as children or young adults painted striking pictures
of the trip. For the many women who were born in the territory,
there were cherished family stories of the trek to the Southwest.

The reasons for coming to Arizona varied, but all had the common theme of a better life. Many came for their health, which
was, of course, tied to the warm climate. Early Mormons came
at the behest of Brigham Young to establish Mormon communities and "make the desert blossom." Some came for the sheer
adventure of trying out life in a young and different land. The
most common reason for settling, however, was economic improvement, both for individuals and families, whether in ranching, farming, mining, teaching, or trade.

Newcomers arriving in the desert were astonished by the land
itself. Some loved it immediately, but more feared the stark landscape and the searing heat. Learning to deal with the land and the
heat occupied a large part of their lives. Access to water and water
rights were critical issues that crossed class and ethnic groups,

and farming and ranching were at a pioneer level. Arizona towns
were devoted to mining or trade, and most were small and relatively undeveloped.

Anne Bush described her young parents' journey to Arizona
from Utah. Her father drove their herd of cattle through Nevada,
and her mother came separately with an infant and a young boy:

✦   ✦   ✦

My mother came across Lees Ferry, which is the most treacher-
ous place in the world for anyone to cross. She never got over
the fear of that crossing. She had this tiny baby just three
months old and the boy who drove the team was only 14 or 15.
It took something like three weeks to get from where they
lived in southern Utah to Apache County. And they got there
in December of 1880 and my father drove the cattle around and
joined them. They had a sack of rice and they had rice, rice,
rice all the time. [They] simply had to live through that winter
[and] sleep in their covered wagon. [In the spring,] they had
to build their own shelter, their own log cabin, and live as best
they could until they could get something growing.[1]

✦   ✦   ✦

In 1914, when Mae Wills was five years old, she and her family
traveled from New Mexico to Arizona by wagon, which took
several weeks. She remembered it as an adventure: "We carried
everything we owned with us. We moved into a little place called
York, near Duncan. It would probably drive people crazy now,
because if you made 15 or 20 miles a day, [you'd do well,] and
you stopped, of course, and we fixed lunch. If it was nice
weather, we put our beds on the ground and slept out. If it was
raining, we had to get in the wagon under the sheet."[2]

Train travel was faster, but not always comfortable. Brenda
Meckler remembers: "We came in September 1918, and it was a
very hot, uncomfortable, difficult trip. We came by coach and the
coach was dirty, it was vermin infested, and it was horrible."[3]
Fern Johnson recalled her parents' trip from Ohio by train. While

they arrived in Arizona relatively quickly, their furniture took two to three months.⁴ Edna Brazill, who traveled from Chicago to Phoenix in 1918 by train, described her first impressions of Arizona: "It just seemed like a haven after riding from El Paso through the desert of New Mexico. In the morning as we approached Mesa and Tempe, [it seemed] all greenery."⁵

Elsie Dunn had perhaps the most adventurous approach to her new home. Her parents came by wagon, drawn by horses, but she rode her mule, refusing to leave it behind. Only seven or eight, she convinced her parents she could ride along with them two hundred miles from the New Mexico border near Duncan, Arizona, to Naco in southern Arizona. She recounted her trip: "We crossed over sand hills and climbed over mountains. I remember I had some awful sores."⁶

Following a typical migration pattern, men in the late nineteenth century often came to Arizona alone, without their wives and children, to begin settling. Once they were established, their families followed. Violet Irving's grandfather first came to the Verde Valley in 1870. Only after he had established a homestead did he come back for his wife and two-year-old son.⁷ Loretto Coles's grandfather followed the western "lure of gold" and immigrated from England to Tombstone to mine in the early 1880s. Her grandmother, who had a "spirit of adventuring," came later with her two-year-old daughter.⁸

Mormon families were an exception to the "male first" settling pattern. Instructed by their church to colonize the desert, they traveled as families, often in groups of families, to form an entire community. Clara Kimball related the story of her family's journey to St. David, Arizona:

✦   ✦   ✦

President Brigham Young was telling the people to go to different places in Arizona and settle and make a way for themselves. He said, "Colonize Arizona. Make it blossom as a rose." He told my parents in a congregation meeting to go down to this place on the San Pedro River, above St. David about seven or eight miles. So [in 1888] they went down there and they secured this property by surveying and by permission. He wanted to build up a place for this growing population that was coming on in the church. And so my father, Joseph Mann Curtis, and his three brothers, William Curtis, Samuel B. Curtis, and Charlie Curtis, all went down there to the San Pedro River with cattle and horses. I believe it was about three months to come down. They went on through the San Carlos range where the Indians had fixed some places for vegetation, little places of their own, and they went on down through Geronimo and Ft. Thomas and on into Pima, Arizona, where St. David is now. And they thought that would be just a good place and they stayed up there and they colonized that place. They started in digging for water for wells.[9]

◆　◆　◆

Some single women, interested in new places, came to Arizona in search of opportunity. Even as a child in Illinois, Edna Brazill knew she wanted to move to Arizona when she grew up. "I had relatives who were pioneers out here and liked it and cousins of mother's who had come out for the winter and come back, and I would sit at their knees and listen to them tell stories about Phoenix. And I said, 'When I grow up, I'm going to teach school and move to Phoenix.'"[10]

Benita Fennemore recalled that her mother, daughter of an ambassador, "liked adventure, having lived in Latin America. She was interested in seeing what this part [of the country was like]. She knew something of the Spanish or Mexican influence here. I think it appealed to her. She came to teach English at Tempe Normal School [in] 1904. And she was also housemother at East Hall, which was the women's dormitory at that time."[11]

Similarly, Madge Copeland, a Black woman, saw moving to Phoenix as "just a fine opportunity to do most anything you could do." Leaving segregated Louisiana, she "was always glad to go to a new place, somewhere I had never been. I like it very much. I'm still here."[12]

Sometimes doctors prescribed a move to Arizona for their patients' health. Areas around Phoenix and Prescott became centers for people with tuberculosis. Fern Johnson's parents came from Ohio in 1907 because her father had tuberculosis. "The doctor said, 'If you want to live and get well, go to Arizona.' [It] was a big step in their lives and one that wasn't very happy."[13]

People varied in their responses to Arizona. The desert especially drew strong reactions—both negative and positive. Describing her first visit to Arizona before settling in to teach on an Indian reservation, Southerner Charlie Daniels remembered: "The train would stop at the station and I would get out and feel the heat and dash back in. During the night it was hot, during the summer it was hot, come in the spring and it was hot. I wasn't accustomed to feeling this kind of heat at night. Sometimes it would be early in the morning, past midnight, and it would still be hot. Hotter than any temperature I had ever been in."[14]

Marjorie Mandel believed that "the desert is something that at first you fear, but then you learn to love it—it's so beautiful."[15] On the other hand, Tillie Garten, who came as a child and was always interested in beautiful things, thought the desert "didn't look exactly too beautiful to me."[16] Echoing Garten, Loretto Coles's grandmother, fresh from England, was "very disappointed" when she arrived in Tombstone. "She didn't realize how arid the country was compared to England and the actual hardships they [would have] coming from a country that was already pretty well settled."[17]

Lyrically making the case for the desert's peculiar beauty, Brenda Meckler, fresh from a farm in Ohio, described her impressions on arrival: "I loved the desert. Someone took us out to the desert at twilight and that did it for me. The canals were everywhere and they were lined with cottonwood trees and at sunset it was lovely. You know how delicate the leaves of the cottonwoods are and they seemed almost detached. Against the sunset they would be like a mass of black lace. The hills were very dramatic. Some people were put off by the desert. They felt it was harsh and ugly, but I never felt that way about it."[18]

Edna Phelps moved to Arizona at the age of nine. Living on a farm in Phoenix, she described rural desert life in the summer season of storms and dust:

✦   ✦   ✦

Most of our rains in those early days came in early July; we could almost [tell what] day it was, because the Fourth of July would be a cloudburst. There would be tremendous lightning, tremendous thunder, and then this downpour of rain. We'd go out and look at the mountains and all those little ravines on the mountains [would be] rushing, bilious, yellow-looking color bringing that silt down to empty into the canal. I never knew the lightning to strike anything nearby, but the thunder-claps would sound like cannon shots and we [would be] a lit-tle terrified. Sometimes a big flood would come in the day-time, but mostly they came in evenings or night.

When they came in the daytime, we'd sometimes have a lit-tle tragedy because the small chickens would be roaming the orchard, which was in the hollow, south of the house and many of them would become super wet and a few would drown. I tried artificial respiration on some of them and man-aged to pump the water out [of] their little ribs and lungs after they seemed to be dead and some of them perked up and ran off and were happy ever after.

One of the things that happened when we'd have those cloudbursts [was that] within half an hour after the floods came, there would be a chorus of frogs just singing and [they would] make the night ring with their songs. I was very curious about this phenomenon because here on the boiling hot desert with no water except when the floods came, there [would be] frogs. They [were] in the banks of the gully and they [could] stay there for years. When the water came, they [would] dig out and reproduce very rapidly. This started then the next cycle of the frogs. The chorus of frogs would last as long as the stream was running.

[Edna's parents allowed the children to swim in the canal when it was clear.] Of course, our parents were much concerned for our safety and well aware of the threats that the canal posed for young children. So to satisfy our wishes to get into the canal and still keep us safe, they mounted a sturdy post on the bank at the point nearest the house. To the post were secured three ropes, one to tie around each of us. What fun we had and what daring adventures for three kids, ages ten, eight, and one just short of six years.

The canal was cold and clear most of the year until the midsummer cloudbursts. The mountain [run-off] would turn it [into] a roiling, yellow, nasty mess, and it smelled bad because all sorts of debris, even dead animals [would] wash into the canal from the north bank. Then for six weeks or so, we just couldn't even go in the canal, we couldn't even hold our nose and go in because it was so polluted.

In addition to the cloudbursts, when we were living on the homestead, July and August would bring every night a great rolling bank of red dust over the northeast mountains. We watched this red bank—it looked slow from a distance, but I know it was roaring along. It would roar over Paradise Valley, then it would engulf Squaw Peak, and then it would be entering our house and it was just a smothering blanket of dust. This would last 30 minutes to an hour and then it would subside. The house was loaded with dust because we had only canvas shutters. Sometimes we didn't get them all down quickly enough to shut it out. Then I remember poor mother the next day patiently sweeping out dust and patiently mopping the floors only to know it would be the same thing the next night. Now, we don't have those dust storms anymore. I have not seen that red bank of dust come over those mountains in twenty years.[19]

✦ ✦ ✦

Arizonans lived in either a rural environment of farming and ranching or a town environment of mining or trade. Often where people lived, either in the country or a town, was the single most important factor in their daily lives.

Most Arizonans were farmers or ranchers. Conditions were fairly primitive and water was a major concern in the desert. The primary cash crops were cotton, grains, and citrus. Cattle and sheep grazed on the range. Sallie Lewis, a Mohave Indian, lived on the reservation when she was a girl. Her father farmed about sixty acres, since each family member was allotted ten acres apiece. Sallie fondly remembers her childhood: "[My father] had cotton, alfalfa, and grain, like wheat and maize, and then [my parents] always had a garden to put their corn and vegetables in. [My mother] took care of the garden and we had people help [with] the rest, like harvesting the grain, hay, and cotton [which] was picked by hand. In the summer we lived out most of the time under the trees. [It was] very hot, but it didn't bother me at the time."[20]

Fern Johnson's parents emigrated from the Midwest and found the living conditions hard, reflecting what they had given up:

✦   ✦   ✦

[They had come] from big families to Phoenix, which was very small. They were out in the country, and it was desert, and it was a very lonely place. And the winds and the sand blew and the snakes were in the chicken's nest, and the coyotes ate the dog food. They bought a farm right close to what is now the main Sears store on Camelback, and that is where I was born on August 14, 1908, one of the hottest months we have. [The farm] was a small place, probably 20 acres, and at that time I don't think they had cattle. They brought their seed along from Ohio and I suppose it was grain. Both of them came from farms in Ohio. Beautiful farms with fruits, vegetables, animals and barns, and big houses. The houses in Arizona were shacks and it was a real letdown.

We sold that farm and we moved [farther out in] the desert [to] a rented farm [with] a little two-room house with no closets and a long porch on the front. It was so rocky that all they did [was run] cattle. We had to carry our water, except when we used ditch water. It was real clean coming over the rocks. We were about half a mile from the Arizona Canal. Of course my mother wept about that because she had been used to a well.

My grandfather came out [to visit] and went back to Ohio
and said, "You should see what Mattie is living in out there in
Arizona!" They kept that house a couple of years. Then we
moved and bought forty acres, and they got the house mother
wanted. From then on they were better [and] they had more
friends. We were in school and, of course, mother was active in
the church so by that time she was adjusted.[21]

✦   ✦   ✦

Benita Fennemore grew up on a ranch outside of Phoenix. The
hard work and uncertainty left her determined to live in a town
when she was an adult, but her family had the natural optimism
of lifelong ranchers:

✦   ✦   ✦

I'll tell you to this day I don't like ranching. I didn't have an
unhappy childhood. I had a very happy childhood. I had very
tender loving parents, but I just remember how hard they
worked. It seemed to me that we never mowed hay that it
didn't rain. In those days if it rained, your hay mildewed.
Maybe you could feed it to livestock or something, but [you
could not] bale it and ship it; it was not first-class hay. It
seemed to me that there was always something disappointing
that happened on the ranch and yet with it all they always
survived and, I would say, were very optimistic that another
year would be better.[22]

✦   ✦   ✦

Benita was not the only one to escape the rigors of farm life by
moving to town. Proving that everything is relative, however,
many of the new emigrants to Arizona towns from other, more
developed areas were surprised at the rustic conditions and lack
of amenities, while others "loved" their new homes at first sight.

Brenda Meckler recounted her arrival in Phoenix. "We walked
down the street and we saw a store and a man standing in the
doorway who looked Jewish. Many new arrivals [like us] looked
for other Jewish people to give them some guidance and advice.
[We lived right downtown.] The street was unpaved, as most of
the streets were, and when it rained people put planks down

across the street or you would sink into mud. I came to love Phoenix because the size was comfortable. You could walk down the street and know almost everybody and if you didn't, you still said, 'Good morning,' just like we used to on the farm."[23]

Globe was a busy mining town. In 1905, Elsie McAlister's mother came to help her sister who was expecting her first child. Elsie recalled: "She didn't like it. She was ready to go back on the next train and I guess it was a pretty rough place because every other building on Broad Street was a saloon, and they had women in the saloons. She wasn't used to that at all and it really upset her a great deal, but she stayed."[24]

Veora Johnson was a young Black woman from the South, just out of normal school. Sent by her school's president to Mesa, Arizona, she was "thoroughly disgusted" by what she found when she disembarked the train:

✦   ✦   ✦

I looked out and saw a very, very small station and a young gentleman came up to meet me. I was only five feet tall and I weighed about 105 pounds and he just couldn't understand how this could be the teacher. We finally convinced each other that he was looking for me and I was Miss Johnson.

We came down the street. Mesa was a very small town at that time. I was so disgusted. I asked him, "When are we going to pass the little town?" and he said, "You already have." Just that short distance, that was it. So the next thing I wanted to know was where I was going to stay. He said, "We'll be there in a little while" and, of course, we did get there. He told me on the way, "It's a two story." But you see my conception of a two story was a colonial type in the South and, of course, when I saw the little attic they had I sank again just a little bit lower.

The housing in Mesa was deplorable because most people had dirt floors. We didn't stay there very long because they [built] a teacherage and that's where we lived. It was the first house that had all the modern conveniences—running water, lights and gas. Of course, that was soothing for this wounded spirit. The school was a two-room brick [building]. I had never seen a school that small in my whole life, because I had gone to a [two-story] red brick school in my own home town as a child. When I saw [the school] I said, "That's where I'm going to teach?" They said, "Yes." What could I do? Here I was and I couldn't let down the president [of my normal school]. He had said I could do it so I came, I saw, I stayed. And here I am.[25]

✦   ✦   ✦

Mary Moeur's family also arrived by train. She exuberantly remembered her first Arizona morning. "We got off the train and my father looked at the people in the station at Tempe and said, 'This is God's country!' I've never seen anyone adore a place as much as my father loved Tempe. It was such a tiny little old place, but we just always felt that we'd come home and we haven't moved since."[26]

Newcomers to Arizona faced two major problems: obtaining adequate water and learning to deal with the heat. People settled where they could find water, built houses with cross ventilation and screened porches, and planted trees as fast as they could. Drinking water often had to be brought to houses from some distance and even canal water for agriculture sometimes had to be taken from the canal to the fields by hand, so early Arizonans were natural water conservationists.

Edna Phelps described how access to water shaped her family's homesteading:

✦   ✦   ✦

Naturally, when we came to the desert, we had to think of water supply. It is quite likely that we would never have homesteaded where we did if it hadn't been [for] cornering the Arizona Canal. The southwest of our quarter section of land fell at that precise intersection and that gave us a swimming pool and water for the livestock, the chickens, the horses, and the cows that we had occasionally. [We] dipped canal water into barrels sitting on a sled that Dad had manufactured and [it was] dragged by Dolly, our faithful mare, up to the house and used for numerous purposes.

For our drinking water, we had been invited to go to a

neighbor who had a well who lived at Glendale Street, just east of 12th Street. The house had been there for some time and he had a huge alfalfa field and some citrus trees and some nice cottonwood trees in the backyard. We were allowed to go with the spring wagon and the horse over there. We would have to drive east of the canal to the 16th Street bridge and down 16th Street to Glendale and back to 12th Street to get to his yard. There we would fill three or four ten-gallon milk cans with water and haul that water back home. This is the water that we used for drinking and cooking. We probably had to haul water twice a week and we were very careful with its use. All other water [we got from the canal and hauled ourselves.]

What joy we experienced along in the 1920s when the dozen or so citrus trees that dad had planted in the lower land would occasionally get a thorough soaking because the canal had risen high enough to overflow. At other times, when a drought was cruelly persistent and the canal just wouldn't rise, [my brother] Louis would stand at the bank of the canal and dip with a bucket by the hour into a small dish that led into the orchard. It was backbreaking work, and I'm sure that his valiant efforts saved the trees on a number of occasions.[27]

✦   ✦   ✦

Arizonans without access to the canals settled near rivers, springs, or washes and often dug for water. Clara Kimball remembered vividly her family digging their first well. "In the beginning, they carried water in barrels from the San Pedro River right up to the ranch. [Then] they struck a lovely big spring of artesian water when I was a young girl. We would just gasp at the big stream of water coming out of those great big pipes. Everybody was just hip-hip-hooray! Everybody was just so glad."[28]

Before electricity, about the only relief people had from the heat was to go outside to the shade of trees, swim in any available water—canals, rivers or lakes—or travel to the mountains or the California beaches. With electricity, people began to use fans and evolve crude evaporative cooling. Fern Johnson described how she coped as a young mother on her farm in Peoria. "We'd move our beds out under the trees at night and when the rain came, we'd move in. I took the babies' beds out in the afternoon in the shade and put wet sheets around them to cool [them] down. People took their little fans to church—every mortuary furnished [them]—and everybody was fanning. [It was] about the only cooling we had."[29]

Elizabeth Hovde explained her attempts to cool her house once she had electricity. "[We built] an apparatus where you could run the water through and get a fan in front and pull the cooler air through. It was just trial and error. One person would improve upon the others and get an idea of their own and so forth. Along in August on a muggy day they were not too successful. That's the reason so many of these old houses have screen porches—it was either sleep on the porch or sleep outside."[30]

Because Arizona was such a rural territory, people often lived in isolation from one another. They had to develop their own resources and many times were challenged by the environment. Women sometimes were lonely and occasionally scared when they were left alone miles from friends and family. Irma West told a humorous story about going as a child to stay overnight with her aunt.

◆   ◆   ◆

In our early years I was called on real often to go different places to stay with women overnight and my mother always let me go. I was painting the benches out on the front porch and getting ready for Sunday School classes when my Uncle Andy drove up and said, "Aunt Belle saw a bear yesterday and she is afraid to stay alone tonight and I have to be gone. Could you come and stay with her on Sunday?" And I said, "Well, yes, I would." Sunday after church all at once my mother said, "Irma, it's getting late. Did you forget?" And I said, "Oh, mother." And she said, "You'll have to run."

So I immediately took off and started to run. I got about half way, and I had to take off my stockings and shoes [to] wade through the creek. I remember my father saying that sometimes the night was so black that you couldn't even see your hand before you. And it was a cloudy night and I took my hands out and I couldn't see [them]. Oh, it was a black night, and the hoot owls [were] hooting and the coyotes were barking. Just a little way up the creek I could hear a lot of sounds but I was in the lane after that and it led up to past the West place and I saw the light in the window, and I'll tell you that I was afraid. There was a little wood gate that I had to take off just about opposite from where the Wests lived and go through a whole big forty acres and over a little hill before I would get to Uncle Andy['s] place. It was approximately two miles from where we lived. As I went through the meadow I had to get down on my hands and knees in order to feel the trail. The cows were grazing on one side and the owls were hooting and those coyotes were barking and I heard way off down the reservation the sound that I knew was a mountain lion. Because I had heard it described; [it was] just like a child crying so pitifully. I was out there where the bear was and I knew Aunt Belle wouldn't come because she was afraid of the bear. Every cow I saw I thought could be that old bear. I got over the last little hill and I saw a light. I thought, "I made it all right!" But all at once a great, big dog was in front of me. I knew my uncle had two big dogs he kept for killing lions. He kept them tied up because they were man killers. And they were growling and their teeth [were] grinding and Aunt Belle heard them and she called out, "Irma, is that you?" And I said, "Yes." She said, "Stand still." Well, I couldn't have done anything else. I just froze in my tracks. She came out and got a hold of the collars of the dogs and she said, "Run!" And I ran to the house and shut the door and I no more than got it shut when the dogs hit the door with their paws and tried to get in. [Aunt Belle] had to go around the house to get in and when she came in, she was as white as a sheet. She said before the week was out Uncle Andy would have to kill those dogs. [Concluding her story, Irma West recollected:] I was called to do many things that were brave and daring. Riding horseback through the trees without a saddle; we just did everything that we could and it was a great life.[31]

◆   ◆   ◆

Late nineteenth- and early twentieth-century Arizona was rough and primitive, and people's responses to the desert varied by their personality and reason for coming. Leaving a beloved and fertile midwestern farm because a family member had "weak lungs" probably made the transition to hardscrabble, waterless homesteading harder than coming at the behest of Brigham Young to make the desert blossom. Likewise, arriving in Tempe by train after a civilized trip from Illinois made it easier to think of "God's country" than riding a mule through the desert for five hundred miles. And a definition of relativity seems to be the description of Tempe as an "oasis, all greenery" made by a young woman after her arrival from El Paso. With each year new people continued to settle, expanding both the rural and town economies. Responding to the desert's unique environment called on both newcomers and natives to conserve water and adapt to the heat. Traditional women's roles were sometimes challenged and expanded, and our women's stories of growing up in Arizona show the ways the Arizona environment shaped their lives.

GROWING UP IN ARIZONA

✦

*My mother's days were very busy. We never had to look
for any work at our house.*   Fern Johnson

All of the women interviewed for this book vividly remembered
growing up in pioneer Arizona where their parents or grandparents raised them, often under difficult conditions. Reminiscing
about their childhoods, the women recounted stories of their
mothers' and grandmothers' hard household labor and the varied
work they all did on farms and ranches. Additionally, they fondly
recalled the games, parties, and community entertainments of
their youth. They had differing experiences if they grew up in
rural areas rather than towns, but all described their mother's
childbirths, family illnesses, and the use of home remedies, indicating the ways women remained the principal healers in Arizona well into the twentieth century.

While all of the women went to school, their experiences differed enormously depending on whether they lived in rural areas
or towns. Some children had to leave home to attend school,
while occasionally an entire family moved to have schools for
their children. Black children experienced legal segregation in
Arizona, while Hispanic, Asian, and American Indian children
went to schools that were segregated by custom rather than by

law. Further, many American Indian children who lived on reservations had to leave home at an early age to attend boarding schools.

Learning about becoming a woman was an integral part of growing up. As girls entered puberty, they were often unaware of why and how they were changing. While girls were taught ladylike behavior and held to strict ideals of what was acceptable for young women, parents often did not instruct their daughters about their changing lives or sexuality.

Born during the thirty years between 1890 and 1920, these women's childhoods spanned the first third of the twentieth century. As they grew, so did Arizona, developing from a rural, pioneer territory to a burgeoning western state.

Benita Fennemore recalled the difficulties her mother faced as a young wife on a rustic Arizona sheep ranch. The daughter of a wealthy, urbane diplomat, she found life fifty miles from Prescott very hard, with "no luxuries." When Benita was a young girl, the family moved to a ranch in Glendale where conditions were still quite primitive. "My mother [cooked] on a wood stove. We had ice delivered once a week [to] the ranch, a 100 pound block at a time. We were never allowed to chip it. It melted so rapidly [and] they wanted to make it last so they wrapped burlap bags over it. Then the milk or anything that had to be kept was kind of tucked in next to the ice, but things didn't keep at all well. My father also built a burlap cooler, which was out on the back porch. They would dampen the burlap as the air would blow through the cooler canvas; it would help to cool the food, but it wasn't too effective."[1]

Edna Phelps' mother moved from city housekeeping to desert ranching at mid-life. In 1912, when Edna was a young girl, her family moved to the desert outside of Phoenix to homestead. "We had no electricity at first, we had no fuel, except kerosene or wood, and very often when dad would be working, [mother] would have to scrounge wood for the heating stove. Actually, the first year or two she cooked with wood. It would be a matter of being out in the desert and finding dead limbs and breaking them up. They were so brittle, they'd break up pretty well. In a few years, we did get a kerosene cook stove, [but] the living was very primitive."[2]

Reflecting on her mother's days at their farm on the reservation outside Parker, Sallie Lewis recalled that she worked both inside and outside of the house. "She would do all the household chores. It took her practically all morning and part of the afternoon if we had a lot of people staying with us. If things eased off in the afternoon, then she would go out into the fields. She helped with whatever. Sometimes in the mornings she would go for a walk if she had something cooking that she could leave. She got up very early, like sunup."[3]

Company was always welcome and a normal part of rural life. A good farm wife was prepared to have guests. "She almost never knew when she was going to have company. They had food on hand and they just expected people to come, and they kept up their standards remarkably well. She kept linen table cloths and napkins for as long as she lived."[4]

Fern Johnson remembered her family's life on a hardscrabble homestead in Phoenix. Her mother's days were full of hard work, and her labor was integral to the family economy.

✦   ✦   ✦

My mother's days were very busy. We never had to look for any work at our house. You had to heat water outside over a bonfire and carry it to your washer and empty it, and do your bread baking and do all your cooking and we always lived quite a long ways from the store. We had no garden because it was too dry. Mother made butter always, and when [she and Dad] had a few cows, they milked their own. Making butter was so time consuming. She took care of her chickens and the only kind of meat I remember eating was chicken.

We had no way to keep meat because we had no iceboxes. It was too extravagant. So we had no cooling and we always had to drink our milk warm. My mother did a lot of canning. Anytime anybody would give her a fruit or they would buy fruit, she would can and can. Mother never canned anything but fruit, jams, and jellies because she didn't have a pressure cooker.

We sold cream. We had a separator in those early days, and I remember going [downtown] with my father and we took in cans of cream. Mother also sold eggs [at] the grocery. She had [a] record of every egg she sold.

On Sunday all the eggs that the chickens laid, she gave that money to the church for tithe. She used to say, "I used to get more eggs on Sunday than I did other days."⁵

❖   ❖   ❖

Partially as a result of her mother's butter and egg money, Fern's family was able to buy ice for refrigeration and keep fresh food longer. "The iceman eventually started coming [with] a big team of horses [and] a big covered wagon of canvas and when he got there a lot of the ice was melted. We'd put it in an icebox and cover it with paper."⁶

Several women recalled that their mothers sold eggs, milk, and butter to supplement the families' incomes. Often the money they acquired made the difference between hard times and some amenities. And selling always involved a trip to town. Clara Kimball exemplified a child's view of the adventure and urban possibilities inherent in taking eggs and butter to market.

❖   ❖   ❖

[Mother] sold lots of chickens, eggs, milk, and butter in Tombstone and Benson and she got money for that. When it would come time to go to Tombstone, she would say, "Now I'll take two of you, but I can't handle more." We went straight to the store [where] they had all kinds of lovely material.

Tombstone was such a big city. It was quite a treat to get to go. Mother would say, "What about us going into the Can Can Restaurant and having something to eat while we're here?" The Can Can Restaurant was a Chinese restaurant and it was a very wonderful place for us. Oh my, to go in a restaurant to eat. So we'd get in there and mother would say, "Now if you would please give these children a bowl of soup and some crackers, it would be just fine." We knew we wouldn't get much else, but the soup, oh my, being in a restaurant and eating that soup. It tasted so wonderful to us. I well remember it. And on the way coming home with one horse, Old Babe, and a buggy. [Before] going home, mother bought a little piece of cheese, or a little piece of baloney. We thought that was oh, so wonderful to eat a little bit on the way going home because it was quite a long ways, about twelve miles.[7]

✦   ✦   ✦

Raised by her grandmother, Violet Irving vividly described her grandmother's daily and seasonal life on a productive farm in the mountains beyond Prescott at the turn of the century.

✦   ✦   ✦

[Grandmother] took care of the milk cow, and some chickens and things like that. If grandfather had just one or two men, she cooked for [those], too. And she kept house. She was a midwife; she brought most of the babies in that part of the country into the world, or helped bring them into the world, and she was a neighbor.

She had a big garden. She always put up a lot of fruit; she made her own yeast cakes and raised vegetables that were put in the cellar for the winter. She was a very, very busy woman but never too busy to make doll clothes for me, sew for me, and visit with me.

She was a beautiful cook, but her stock expression when I wanted to learn how [was], "Oh, I can do it while I'm telling you." I learned afterwards that she was just too busy to stop and tell a youngster how to cook something. And, of course, those women did not cook from recipes. They just took it out of the cupboard and poured it in, and it's a little hard to try to teach somebody how to cook [like that].

She picked wild grapes and we had apples. We got peaches

from other people who lived where it wasn't quite so high
in the mountains and cold. She canned and made jam, and we
had a big cellar. Some of the vegetables were put in the cellar.
Root vegetables [were put in] a long, deep trench lined with
straw. Cabbages would be pulled up root and all, and the
cauliflower leaves would be tied over that, and the carrots and
turnips, and things like that. The parsnips were left in the
ground because the frost doesn't hurt them. They were put in
[the trench with] more straw and then a big mound of dirt over
the top of that so the frost didn't go through. About once
every two weeks, grandfather would dig a hole and pull out
enough to do my grandmother for a couple of weeks. He knew
where each vegetable was [because] he put them in.

My grandfather smoked our pork. Grandmother made
sausage, fried it, and we had great big crocks, and she'd put a
layer of these sausages in a crock and pour the rendered lard
over the top of it and then another layer. Each one of those
layers was sealed, and they stayed fresh the whole winter. Of
course, they were kept in the cellar where it was cold.[8]

✦　✦　✦

Involved in her community as a midwife and "neighbor," with
all the duties that being a good neighbor entailed, Violet's grandmother, an active farm wife, nevertheless stopped every day for
the ritual of tea. Taught by an "old English maiden lady" on her
parents' ranch when she was a girl:

✦　✦　✦

She had learned to make her afternoon tea. My grandfather
always came in no matter what he was doing and always took
off his work shirt and put on a clean shirt and my grandmother
took off her apron and made herself much more presentable
each afternoon at four o'clock when they had tea. The neighbors
all knew that my grandmother had tea about four o'clock in
the afternoon, so usually somebody dropped in. She'd probably
take a half an hour from a busy time of the day, but that was

their time to visit and relax. As long as she lived, she did that. She had her tea at four o'clock in the afternoon.[9]

✦　✦　✦

Cecelia Sneezy was also raised by her grandmother, but the conditions were very different from Violet Irving's. As San Carlos Apaches, they lived on the reservation. Cecelia described her childhood.

✦　✦　✦

I was taken care of by my grandmother. She got the ration food, different kinds of flour, bacon, a can of tomatoes, corn and beans, and green coffee that my grandma used to roast. I was raised poor.

We were so poor one time, we were about seven and I was the oldest, about 15. Our grandma got sick. We had to boil beans and it got spoiled. Still we [had to] eat that, [it had a] kind of foam on top of it. That was it; we didn't have any [other] food. She was in the hospital and we were by ourselves.

It was hard. I'd even go out with my grandma to get some wood sticks to get a fire, make food, and cook [and we would gather] acorn, mulberry or scale.[10]

✦　✦　✦

Every woman remembered childhood activities clearly, but none captured their attention like laundry. Among all the chores and jobs women and girls had to do, laundry stood out: a task larger than all the rest and one that was continual, week in and week out. Every woman described her mother's wash day in detail, even the ones who otherwise said little about daily chores, and not one was sorry to see the washboard go, although many reflected wistfully that sun dried sheets glistened white and smelled wonderful. "On the day mother designated as wash day, dad was up at daybreak to build the outdoor fire under the wash tub. Mother had chiseled a bar of soap into this water since that was before the days of detergent. A prize bit of fuel for the heat under the boiler was an old automobile tire that might be found discarded on the desert and what a roaring fire it made. We watched with fascination the voluminous billows of black sooty smoke roll off into the wide blue yonder."[11]

Benita Fennemore remembered both washing and ironing:

✦   ✦   ✦

The washtub was built up on a wooden bench, a platform, and you just stood over the washboard and scrubbed and carried hot water. My father would usually arrange to help mother lift the [tubs], carry out the hot water or carry out the cold water to rinse the things in. To this day I still love the smell of clothes when they are hung on the line to dry.

In order to iron they had to have this big wood stove going again. They had these old-fashioned flat irons with the wooden handles that clamped on and you'd iron and then when you got through, you'd unclamp it and put it back on the stove so it could reheat, and you'd take a fresh iron to iron. And you'd usually sprinkle these clothes the night before and roll them up in something. It seems to me there was always ironing. I think my mother tried too hard to keep us presentable.[12]

✦   ✦   ✦

Women who lived in towns had somewhat easier lives than farm and ranch women. There were always neighbor women to help with difficult times and daily visiting was possible. All towns had women's clubs, churches, and ladies auxiliaries, as well as other social institutions. Stores were also close at hand, and butter and other locally made foodstuffs could be bought every day. Middle class or wealthy town women also could hire household help to ease the burden of housework, cooking, and laundry.

Elsie McAlister described her mother's day in Globe in the teens:

✦   ✦   ✦

We all came home for dinner [at mid-day] including my father. That was the big meal of the day. [Mother] did a lot of sewing— she loved to sew. She always took a nap in the afternoons. And then later she joined a women's club and that was very enjoyable. They would sit around in the neighborhood and help people. In those days it seems that people did visit a great deal more than they do now. If there was a newlywed in the neighborhood, very often they would go over and teach her their specialty in cooking. They would leave the recipe for her, which was very thoughtful and very nice. And if anyone was sick they took care of them at home; the neighbors took care of anyone who was ill.

There was a colored woman here in Globe who came during Christmastime and served our big dinners. She did practically all the cooking and she very often did the family wash and ironing. And then there were two or three other people who would come in the house and do those things until electric washing machines came along [and] that ended.[13]

❖   ❖   ❖

Definitions of women's work varied. Loretto Coles remembered her mother's busy life in Bisbee. The wife of a large store owner, Mrs. Coles "[would] get up in the morning and order all the groceries. She almost always had help. She didn't have to actually do the scrub work, but she had to plan meals and she had a social life, too. The help came from miners' wives. A lot of them were Swedish. And they were excellent, handy girls."[14]

At home in Sonora, Arizona, Ruby Estrada's mother had ten children, six of whom were born in seven years. She recalled that her mother "always had help. She used to send out her washing and there was always someone there to help her."[15]

The wife of a hardware and furniture store owner, Mrs. Lopez was suddenly widowed in 1926 at the age of 37, with ten children, the oldest of whom was eighteen. She took over the store and raised the children. "That's the only place she worked, but it was our own store. She acquired it out of necessity. Everything was necessity. Until my father died she never worked. He had men working for him. She must have been very smart. When she took it over she never did think of that, just took it from there."[16]

All of the girls had household chores and helped their mothers, learning how to perform women's traditional work. Girls whose families ran businesses often helped there, too, like Ruby Estrada, who worked in the hardware store after her father died. Farm and ranch girls also had important outdoor chores, such as feeding the chickens and working in the garden. Additionally, they helped with the harvest. Clara Kimball recounted:

✦   ✦   ✦

When it was haying time we would go and help get the hay in. The men would get the hay all cut and then we girls would oftentimes rake the hay ourselves. [We also would help harvest the wheat.] We would follow behind and we had aprons on. Mother would go right along with us and we would pick up all these heads of wheat and put them in our apron. Mother would then go dump them into the machinery that whips the wheat out. It was lots of fun. Another thing that we did was bring in loads and loads of hay on a hayrack. When we'd get to the barn the menfolk would take this old mule to the barn. After the hay got about four or five feet high they'd put [the] old [mule] up there, and then we girls would just have lots of fun riding him around in the top of the barn.[17]

✦   ✦   ✦

Girls often rode and were likely to help with cattle on ranches. Elsie Dunn remembered, "I would get on my horse and bring in the cows [from] the pasture. I [helped] milk the cow[s] and brought the cans to the house. Then I helped feed the calves and take care of them. I loved to be outside."[18]

Clara Kimball helped with her family's beekeeping:

✦   ✦   ✦

We girls always extracted [the] honey. We would put the slats of honey outside the extractor and whip the honey out. We'd put a can down underneath the faucet on the outside and drain all of the honey off. [In] just a day or two we'd have gallons and gallons of honey [to sell]. We would make vinegar out of [the leftover honeycombs. The first step in making vinegar is the fermentation of honey and water into mead.] Sometimes the Indians would come down when we were making vinegar. [The mead] was a real good drink; it would get them real drunk. We all liked to drink it, too, but not when it was bad enough to make any of us drunk, because we never liked it that way. We didn't want any of our family to get drunk on it.[19]

◆   ◆   ◆

Another important aspect of women's work was their families' and communities' health care. Women were the primary midwives and healers—some were formally trained and others learned by doing. Regardless of their level of training, they delivered most of the babies in Arizona and took care of the sick in their communities. While doctors provided medical care and attended births in some of the larger towns, especially mining towns where they were hired by the mine owners at hospitals and clinics owned by the mines, most Arizonans were cared for by women healers. Mexican women were particularly valued as midwives. Elsie Dunn's mother had nine of her ten children in New Mexico and Arizona with the help of Mexican midwives.[20]

In Mormon communities women were trained, sometimes with church funds, to be healers and midwives for entire communities. Clara Kimball remembered her community's midwife as "Aunt." "Aunt Rhoda S. Merrill, came up to the ranch on horseback [to] wait on [mother] and others around in the woods [who were] having their babies. She was midwife and doctor, took the place of both, and in fact she was doctor to all of mother's children that were born there in San Pedro. She was a very lovely, stately looking lady, and she rode horse real well and she carried her suitcase right along with her on the horse."[21]

Ranch women who lived far from neighbors sometimes came to town to await birth. Benita Fennemore's mother left her ranch and came down to Phoenix. "That's why I was born at the Adams Hotel. In the summertime, my parents were so isolated, so far from town, and this being the first baby, my father was very concerned about my mother having the best possible medical care. As the time approached, he said, 'I think you'd better go down to Phoenix and stay at the Adams Hotel.' There simply was no other place where she could get the medical care that she could get here in Phoenix."[22]

Tuberculosis was a particularly common and difficult illness in the early twentieth century. Arizona became known as a healthy place for tuberculosis patients, and many moved to the desert to try to get well. Despite this belief in the healthy, dry desert air as a preventative against TB, however, many native Arizonans contracted the disease themselves. Tuberculosis was especially prevalent among American Indians in Arizona, and government doctors on the reservation found TB their main health concern.

Sallie Lewis and her older brother and sister all contracted tuberculosis on the reservation. Being Mohave Indians, they were treated by government doctors in hospitals. Sallie recalled: "Edith, my second sister, spent most of her time in the hospital. They had a sanitarium in Phoenix. People had to be taken care of, so that's where she spent most of her time. I didn't know her too well. My brother was there too. And they [both] died."[23] Some years later, Sallie also contracted TB and was sent to the tuberculosis hospital, where she was cured.[24]

Cecelia Sneezy came down with tuberculosis in early adolescence on the Apache reservation in the early thirties. She was treated at home and had to quit school. "They gave me cod-liver oil that really tastes bad. That helped me and I was all right." In the 1970s, Mrs. Sneezy suffered a bad TB relapse and had to take a leave from her job to recover.[25]

Generally, mothers and grandmothers had home remedies for various illnesses and complaints. Some grew herbs and others collected desert plants to make teas and syrups for colds, influenza, and other ailments.

Recalling her mother's skill, Clara Kimball reminisced:

✦   ✦   ✦

Mother liked herbs a great deal and we used a lot of herbs. We had peppermint and catnip planted around our place. Mother always made cinnamon tea for us if we looked like we needed something for a laxative and that was one of her real good remedies. [She] gave us peppermint tea for cramps in our stomach.

Every once in a while, mother would get a little flask of brandy that we'd use for real bad colds, and she said that it would be as good as anything we could use. I know that she used that as medicine every once in a while. Otherwise none of my folks used any kind of liquor [because we were Mormon].

Mother used a lot of vinegar and a lot of salt. She used a lot of old-fashioned liniments I know. My father would find a lot of Almanac remedies.[26]

+   +   +

Fern Johnson also remembered:

+   +   +

We tried many home remedies before we ever went to a doctor. We used castor oil and salt. When anybody was going to get a cold, the first thing we had was a big dose of either one or both. That really washed it out of us. We used kerosene for disinfectant. I don't ever remember having an infection. Some people used turpentine, but we were kerosene people. And then we began to make our own [remedy] from the greasewood leaves on the desert. We picked them and dried them and made a tea. We always rubbed mustard oil or something on our chests.

I can remember [mother] making salve for burns and cuts and things, and the only thing that I remember that went in it was pine pitch, which I learned since I have grown older is very healing, particularly mixed with some kind of fat or something. It smelled, as I can remember, like camphor. What all was in it, I have no idea.

If you had a cold, [you took] a hot glass of lemonade. Sometimes [you] put your feet in mustard water while you're drinking it and then you get in bed, [and] stay there. From my Seventh Day Adventist aunt we learned to use cold packs. And many a time when I had a sore throat and I'd get up and put a cold cloth on my neck and wrap towels around it, in the morning the sore throat would be gone. She even saved a man with a heart attack with her cold packs. So we were great ones for home remedies. We seldom went to a doctor.[27]

✦   ✦   ✦

Even with very serious diseases, when individuals had to be quarantined, mothers often used home remedies and usually nursed their patients at home. Clara Kimball described her mother nursing her younger sister who had diphtheria:

✦   ✦   ✦

They had to isolate her from the rest of the family, put her off in another room. And mother would take care of her there and change her own clothes when she would go out amongst the other children so they wouldn't be contaminated or get the disease.

Mother got the best health care that she could, but they just treated her with home remedies. They were great on home remedies.[28]

✦   ✦   ✦

In 1918 the flu epidemic swept Arizona. More than 400,000 people died nationwide, and every woman remembered the extraordinary steps their communities took to deal with the epidemic locally. People wore masks, most public events were canceled, and schools and theaters all over the state were closed. Emergency hospitals were set up and women were called on to nurse in every community. Even though she was pregnant, Loretto Coles's mother "went out among the miners in Bisbee, cooking food and helping the ones that lost their children and wives."[29] When the hospital in Globe was full, "they opened up East Globe School as an infirmary, and they had to build a special kitchen on the outside of the building. They staffed it with nurses and equipment like a hospital, but they just died right and left."[30] Elsie McAlister's father transported sick people from Miami to Globe in the back seat of his car, "because they did not have any ambulances in the district at that time and it was just up to the individual people in the community to do that."[31] During the epidemic in Phoenix, Edna Brazill remembered "as many as twenty-two caskets stacked up one on top of the other in the [Whitney] mortuary" where her fiancé worked.[32]

In Lakeside, a Mormon community, Irma West recalled what it was like to have the flu. She was 22 and a young married woman. Her mother was expecting a new baby and was afraid of getting the flu because "women mostly died if they delivered babies during the epidemic."[33] Irma's father and mother-in-law took care of her and her family.

✦   ✦   ✦

Grandma West didn't get it. Grandpa West didn't get it. Grandma West said, "I can't get it. I have to take care of my children." And Mother West was not too well with rheumatism, but she got over it. Believe you me, she was out taking care of those babies from one house to another.

Grandpa West was busy seeing that we had wood. We all had to stay in bed. If we got up, we would have a setback. There was a lady who came in with big kettles full of tapioca pudding and rice puddings and some vegetables cooked and different things. And the neighbors that were well were taking care of those that were sick. We had a cousin, oh, she was such a faithful person. She didn't have it. She came in and did our washing and took care of our babies for us, once a week anyway.[34]

✦   ✦   ✦

And Irma West's mother had her own special remedy to protect her family from the flu: "She had lots of onions and they didn't have the flu hardly at all. She would feed them a lot of onions every day. She'd make up a big onion stew or she'd sauté these onions and fry them and fix them some way. So they'd eat lots of onions and they got through the flu [epidemic] with scarcely no trouble at all."[35]

Children's entertainment in pioneer Arizona was largely determined by whether they lived on isolated farms or ranches, in farm communities, like Lakeside or Laveen, or towns, such as

Phoenix or Globe-Miami. About the only amusements common to all groups were Sunday visiting and desert picnics. Children on farms and ranches and their occasional visitors played relatively simple games, which were often outdoors. Children in farm communities had some organized activities, such as hayrides or swimming parties. Especially by the teens and twenties, town children had institutionalized recreation organized by such groups as the Young Women's Christian Association (YWCA), the Girl Scouts, churches, and schools. They also had access to dance halls, theaters, parks, and swimming pools.

Irene Bishop recalled that on her ranch

◆ ◆ ◆

we didn't have playmates. Families would get together on weekends, usually on Sundays. We would go out on the desert and have picnics or would go to someone's home. The men liked to play cards, and the women just visited or sewed or crocheted. During the week, we didn't have too many friends because the farms could be from a half-a-mile to maybe a mile apart. We couldn't call people, so my mother would take the horse and buggy and take us [to] spend the day with someone. That was wonderful. And people would come to spend the day with us; you took it for granted people were home [and] usually they were.[36]

◆ ◆ ◆

Describing the ranch child's day, Fern Johnson explained: "I had a doll and a little stove and I played with my brothers. We played in the ditch out front and in the afternoons we'd make castles and dog houses and climb trees. Sometimes we played in the cotton fields in the daytime. It would be cool, maybe damp. And we played in the sand, of course. We helped with things. We had rabbits. We fed the chickens and baled the hay. And when I got big enough, I had to help dress the chickens. And I don't know, I don't remember people being bored around our house."[37]

As a teenager, Clara Kimball and her brothers and sisters had parties in their home: "We'd invite the neighbors in and have all kinds of games. When I was growing up we had lots of kissing games. We had post office and plant the plow on both sides. All of us would get on a long seat, then we'd join arms and kiss the boy on the left and the girl on the right and back and forth clear down the row. And that was planting the plow on both sides."[38]

Young girls were often taught to play musical instruments, especially the piano, for their enjoyment and that of their families. It was common to find pianos even on isolated farms and ranches. Edna Phelps remembered longing to own a piano, which they could not afford. The children banded together to earn piano money:

✦   ✦   ✦

We pick[ed] cotton and sav[ed] pennies and managed to make a down payment on a secondhand piano in about 1918 or 1920. Part of our money-raising effort was we learned that there was a bounty [of] five cents each for pairs of jackrabbit ears.

The jackrabbit ears accumulated and when we got twenty, we had a dollar. The dollar went toward the piano. I don't remember just how many dollars we had, maybe one or two, from the saving of jackrabbit ears.[39]

✦   ✦   ✦

The Curtis family had a piano and young Clara was encouraged to learn to play. A fine musician, ultimately she became a music teacher with college training. Clara described learning to play the piano and entertaining as a teenager on various occasions:

✦   ✦   ✦

My father wanted me so much to learn to play church songs. He got a hymn book for me and I worked and worked on the hymns so that I could play them. I was the Sunday School organist when I was 10 years old. I was the only organist they had for a long period all through the San Pedro.

The Indians would come down from Ft. Huachuca to get

food for [them and] their horses. The Indians could hear music in the house. They oftentimes came by the windows and they would come peek their heads in and try to listen. Father would go and give them a punch and say, "Well, go on in the house and listen to her play." They would come in the house and sit down around the piano on the floor and I would practice my lesson or play for them and they were highly elated over that. This one fellow enjoyed it so much that he'd take the beads off his own neck and put them over onto my neck and I was highly elated. That pleased me so much that I decided that I'd play some more for them. I played a lot for the Indians. Every time they came down, they wanted me to play.

[When I was 16] I played piano with an elderly gentleman who played violin. The cowboys around here liked old Jim Christianson's music and so they asked him to go up in the Dragoon Mountains and play for the dances. They had a schoolhouse where they had really good hoedowns and Brother Christianson [who was a Mormon family friend] would call and have me go with them to the dance. When midnight came, they would have coffee and cake and rest a little and start playing again until morning.

Another time we went up in the mountains [to] the Russelville Terminal. They had a big supper and the cowboys and all the cowboys' wives and sweethearts had a great big party. On New Year's they started in quite early and danced until way late in · the morning, until the sun was up. My brother and his girl went along with us and they had a great time. It was lots of fun and excitement. The cowboys liked me. One or two of them liked me quite well, and they would come up and pat me on the shoulder and Brother Christianson would just go on with his violin and play something while this cowboy and me would dance around the circle.[40]

✦   ✦   ✦

Teenagers in the farm community of Lakeside organized dances and hayrides. Irma West recalled: "When it was time to go to a dance, the boys would come and gather the girls. They'd take a big wagon and one of the boys would drive the team. The girls and boys without having dates would get in the wagon or two wagons, whatever it took, and they'd sit crossways in the bottom in the hay or straw and in the winter they would put hot rocks to keep us warm and we'd just cover ourselves."[41]

Town kids lived close to each other and could visit every day and play after school. They played in groups and often organized real games. "There were lots of boys and girls in the neighborhood. We all played ball out in the street. The boys in the neighborhood trapped. Oftentimes the girls would pack a little lunch and go and see what they had in their traps."[42]

Living in the mining community of Morenci, Elizabeth Hovde remembered Girl Scout meetings, movies, and Young Men's Christian Association (YMCA) activities:

✦   ✦   ✦

[I was a Girl Scout] about five or six years. We met on the same evening [as] the Boy Scouts. They'd have their meeting and we'd have ours. Then we'd all play together, usually on the tennis courts. Many times they took us on picnics, and it was always the boys and the girls. The thing I liked best is how delicious a hot dog is on stick roasted over the coals, in a bun and mustard with a bottle of soda pop. Most of the time we'd have marshmallows toasted the same way. That was the basic refreshment. We'd go on campouts and different places. The girls didn't go on camping trips the same weekend [as the boys], but otherwise it was basically both.

[Our] parents said that they never worried about a child until they left Morenci because everything was just so automatic. There was a movie twice a week. When that was over, the YMCA stayed open long enough for you to go get some ice cream or something like that. And then it closed down and we went home. [There] wasn't anything else to do. They knew exactly how long it took you to get home and [we were] easy to keep track of. We walked. There was this huge auditorium and the YMCA had dances, and a lot of them were very, very nice. The Masons would have theirs on Washington's birthday and it would be a formal. One year they shipped $300 worth of roses to decorate the building.[43]

✦   ✦   ✦

In Phoenix, Benita Fennemore described her favorite teenage activities:

✦   ✦   ✦

By the time I was in high school, one of the popular places was Riverside Park on South Central Avenue just off the river. They had a marvelous recreation area, a great big Olympic-sized swimming pool, a great big slide, a great big diving tower, places for picnics, and adjacent to the park was a big bandshell where they brought excellent bands. It was very popular. In those days I was permitted to go to that if I was properly chaperoned. And we didn't resent chaperones. But seven or eight of us would all sit together at a big table or booth around the dance floor. Churches were active in promoting student activity also. The Mormon Church always had dances and their dances were chaperoned. Trinity Cathedral, where I attended church, had Saturday night dances which were very popular with the high-school kids.[44]

✦   ✦   ✦

Arizona children all went to schools of one form or another. Families valued schooling, and some even moved to allow their children to have secondary educations. The level of schooling children attained, however, often depended on race, ethnicity, and class, and children's experiences in school often depended on those variables, as well. Students were not necessarily graded by age in the early days; rather, they were more likely to be placed in the grades by accomplishment. There was no uniform starting age for school, nor was there a standard school leaving age.

The small, rural elementary school was the most common in Arizona. Children all over the territory, and later the state, began their educations there. They were nearly as likely to be in a private house or on someone's private land as they were on public property, because individual families often organized the schools, which many times predated public school districts.

Clara Kimball's story was typical of this early school experience:

✦   ✦   ✦

School was about two miles south of the ranch house. I didn't go until I was eight years old; but I had to walk when I went, and it was a long way. We were [not] up there very long because an earthquake came and destroyed that school. The thing was made out of adobe, and it fell down and interfered with the teacher while she was giving a lesson. [We] had to quit that school, and [we] didn't have any place to go. So [my parents] brought the school children [to our property] and we had school in the honey house for awhile until they could get a schoolhouse built north of the house. All of the people went there to school, and we had church and all of the auxiliaries in that building [and] quite a few dancing parties.[45]

✦   ✦   ✦

By the time their children finished elementary school, families in rural areas without nearby high schools had to make choices about whether or not to continue schooling their children. Sometimes children had to leave home to go to high school, sometimes whole families moved, and sometimes children stopped school.

Violet Irving described her schooling from her ranch in Walker: "Grade school in Walker was a real small one-room school house. One teacher taught everybody and we came from several miles around, and during recess we all played baseball—girls, boys, and all if we had enough to play. In bad weather when it was snowing, the teacher read to us much of the time for which we were all hungry. Then I went to St. Joseph's Catholic school. It was a day and boarding school. It was the only place for girls to go in those days. And I boarded there for about two years."[46]

Irma West's family kept their ranch and educated their children in Snowflake, twenty-four miles away: "Father built a little house in Snowflake next to the high school. [My brother and sisters and I] stayed there. We shared it with the principal. We lived in one room and he in another."[47]

Anne Bush's family gave up their homestead to move close to a high school. "Because there wasn't any secondary school in Apache County, my parents moved to Thatcher in southern Arizona for the purpose of getting their [children] in the [Gila Academy], which was maintained by the Mormon Church. They had this whole bunch of boys and my one sister [who] was high school age."[48]

Town families, and families near towns, had more easily available options. Benita Fennemore, who lived on a ranch in Glendale, was able to commute to Phoenix Union High School. "My freshman year in high school I came in from Glendale on a streetcar every morning and went home every evening. It was just great because I did my homework and studying, an hour coming and an hour going."[49]

For American Indian children in Arizona, schooling was often difficult. Many times children had to go away from their families to boarding school at a very young age, and parents sometimes felt they had little ability to choose what they wanted for their children. Education was conducted in English, and in some schools students were punished for speaking their native language. In the early days, and well into the twentieth century, teachers were predominately Anglo and often had values that differed from their young students. Especially at the beginning of schooling, Indian students were likely to experience real culture shock.

Sallie Lewis, a Mohave Indian, told the story of her schooling from age six through high school:

◆ ◆ ◆

I went to school at the age of six and boarded. It was a government school only about three miles from La Mesa. I didn't go home. I didn't like it very well, but I took it, that's all. It's a way of life. I learned English when I went to school. At that time we were all Mohave, [so] we could speak to each other and translate. I think we learned English pretty fast because I don't remember ever wondering what's being said or talked about or anything. [Our teachers were] all Anglo [and] mostly women. I had only one man in the 5th grade.

We could speak Mohave [in school]. They weren't hard [on us]. I've heard of other people saying that they were hard on them and wouldn't allow them to speak their own language, but they didn't seem to do that to us. We had to learn English, and we learned it without too much pressure. I think it all depended on the teacher and how they felt about it. I had so many girls to play with, made so many friends, and we had fun together. My first few days I guess I was sort of lost, but it wasn't too bad because we shared things with each other. We talked and shared things together, and then a little girl [told] us what to do, like using the bathrooms, and washing, and helping us to adjust to the change.

Then at the age of maybe 14, I went away to another boarding school [in Tucson]. I went up to the eighth grade. I was in the sixth grade when I went there. I stayed there three years. You had to go away to school somewhere.

[My parents] felt I should go to a mission school. You had your choice of going [to the BIA Indian School in Phoenix] or Riverside, California. Our doctor had a lot to do with the decision. Since we had tuberculosis in our family, she felt that I should go to a drier climate and Tucson was the place. She encouraged them to send me there.

I didn't have any [Anglo friends] because we didn't have any around. In the school they didn't have any either. When I went to the boarding school, it was all Indian, so I didn't have any [Anglo friends] until I went to [Farm] High School [in Tucson]. We were friends, the Black and the Spanish and the white people.

The first year [at Farm High School] I was shy. There were so many students. A few of us girls were friends from the [boarding] school and the church had a house and we had a housemother and about ten of us stayed there about a block away from the high school. The first year was rather different, but I had my Indian friends so that helped. We got along and after that we made friends with others.[50]

✦   ✦   ✦

Cecelia Sneezy, an Apache Indian, went to a day school, because her grandmother refused to send her away:

✦   ✦   ✦

I lived in a tepee with my grandma. When I was seven years [old the authorities] wanted me to go to public boarding school. [They] forced [students] to go over there, but grandma and grandfather said we don't want you to go there, cause lots of kids go and play outside, you know, dancing. They said, "I don't want you to do 'that.'" So, they sent me down to mission school.

I learned from the Bible and everything about how to live a good life, how to behave. I go to school there until I got sick.

I go home [every day]. We don't have transportation [at] that time so that is when my grandmother and grandfather moved and we lived close to the school and church. We moved back up with father, and there is other boys and girls that come even from San Carlos. We walk down on [the] railroad [tracks]. I make a perfect attendance even when I walk to school, but I didn't finish.[51]

✦   ✦   ✦

Hispanic children did not have to move away to attend school, but they usually went to schools segregated by custom where they had to speak English, regardless of the primary language they used at home. Ruby Estrada remembered: "[In grade school, the teachers] were very biased. All we spoke was Spanish, and if you didn't speak [English] then they would send you to the office and they were very mean that way. They never did get me, but they used straps, they were cruel. The teacher was mean, then the kids got mean."[52]

Black children in Arizona went to schools that were segregated by law from the teens until 1953, a year before the 1954 Supreme Court decision in *Brown v. Topeka School Board*, which desegregated public schools nationwide. Some communities seemed to elect a kind of extralegal local option, however, and resisted segregation when there were only a few Black students in a school district.

When Irene King's family moved to the Phoenix area in 1920, Irene attended several different elementary schools, all of which had different segregation policies.

◆   ◆   ◆

In 1920 my father moved and asked the fellow he was working for, "Where will my children go to school?" The man said, "Send them on down to Madison" [which was a white school]. My first week at a school was at Madison. They immediately made arrangements for us to take the streetcar and come back into Phoenix to the Black school [Phoenix Elementary #1].

They had a state law. They had to provide separate schools. Some districts we went with the whites. They said separate schools and maybe they had one Black, so they just hung up a sheet. Now if anyone from the state department walked in this little person knew how to go behind that sheet. Then they were separated. Quite a few districts did that. [They provided their separate facility on the other side of the sheet,] as long as somebody was checking it. If no one was checking on them, they just went [with the rest].

We had a problem with segregation [in Laveen also]. [If] they didn't have enough Black children to have separate schools, we had to be transported, and that's why I went to Roosevelt School two different years. The Laveen District just transferred us up there.

When I was in the eighth grade, I was the only one from the Laveen District to be transferred.

When we moved here in 1920, they had put on four Black teachers at Phoenix Union. They put in some cabins and that's where the Blacks went under these Black teachers.

By the time my oldest brother was attending Phoenix Union, they moved [Blacks] off the Phoenix Union campus. They had

a great big house on 9th Street and Jefferson where they moved
the Black school. My sister started [at] what they called Phoenix
Union Carver School at 5th and Grant, and my brother was
one of the first students there.

I have fought segregation for years because I resented it. We
[had] to use an old Chevy to come to high school, and the
whites had a school bus. They would pass by us and laugh
because they were on the bus. There was always quite a bit of
humiliation.[53]

✦   ✦   ✦

Students at segregated schools had their own activities that
were separate from white schools. Minority students who attended classes in primarily Anglo schools, however, often were
not allowed to participate in community activities with their
classmates. The Black high school in Phoenix, for instance, had
a full roster of clubs, dances, sororities, and fraternities that made
it possible, as Irene King recalled, to attend "quite a few affairs"
and still avoid "ventur[ing] out in the community."[54] By contrast, Susie Sato, a Japanese-American student at an Anglo high
school, recounted an incident she experienced in 1934:

✦   ✦   ✦

When we were graduating high school it was customary for the
senior class, at Mesa High School, anyway, to have a day
called "ditch-day" . . . And on ditch-day we went to the Tempe
Public Swimming Pool to have our picnic there. Unfortunately,
we were not allowed . . . in the pool. There were two other
Orientals, I believe, and . . . there were three Mexican students
and one Black student in our graduating class. I don't recall
whether the Black student was there or not, but anyway, we
were turned away. I was with five of my . . . [Anglo] friends.
And they were really very much surprised, and they felt badly
about it, but there wasn't anything that we could do about it.[55]

✦   ✦   ✦

Post-secondary education for women in Arizona was available from as early as 1885 at Tempe Normal School, later Arizona State Teachers College, and soon after at the University of Arizona, Northern Arizona Normal School, and various business and technical colleges. Occasionally, students left the state to attend college, especially for specific professional training. Families' beliefs about education for women and also their economic standing had a great deal to do with whether or not women were able to go on to post-secondary school. For most middle-class women, regardless of ethnic or racial background, professional education, especially to teach, was relatively common. Many women from working-class or relatively poor rural backgrounds saw post-secondary training as a way to open up work opportunities and improve their positions. Despite its pioneer status in the period from 1885 to 1920, Arizona presented real opportunities for women's post-secondary education, which have continued until the present day.

Some women had difficulties in persuading their fathers that women's education was worthwhile. Exie Zieser wanted to become a schoolteacher, but her parents would not allow her to leave home. Her mother supported her aspirations to go to business college, however, and "finally convinced" her father. "It was the best thing I ever did in my life," she recalled later. "I didn't have to clean houses and do things for other people. I can do all kinds of office work."[56]

Ruby Estrada, whose father was dead, was sent to college by her mother over the strong objections of her maternal grandfather:

❖   ❖   ❖

My grandfather thought [girls] had enough education. He figured they were going to get married. I have an aunt [two years older than I, who] got a scholarship and he wouldn't let her go to the University of Arizona. Everybody begged him: the principal, the superintendent, everybody, the teachers. They even offered to lend him money. He had the money. It wasn't that he didn't have the money, he just didn't believe in women [getting an education]. Up to this day Carmen still thinks about it. [She wouldn't go on her own against his wishes.][57]

✦   ✦   ✦

Detailing her educational background, Irene Bishop described her experiences at Tempe Normal School beginning in 1912:

✦   ✦   ✦

I went six years to the old Kyrene School, and then I went two years to Rural School, which was where I graduated from eighth grade. Then I went to Normal School [for] a five-year course. I had to drive a horse and buggy six miles to school. I never missed a class.

There were eight buildings on the campus. There was one boys' and one girls' dormitory, a dining hall, the president's home, Old Main, the auditorium, a training school, and science building. We would unhitch the horse and leave it in a lane where Hayden Library is now. The horses had to stand there all day.

All classes except our science class were held in the Main Building. At the east end of the first floor was the library and study hall where each of us had an old-fashioned desk. The library was in the same building, and that way we could leave our books in between classes. We didn't have to walk all over the campus like people do now going to school.

I [knew] it was quite a sacrifice for our parents to send us all through school, and I wouldn't have thought of dropping out.[58]

✦   ✦   ✦

In 1925 Tempe Normal School became Arizona State Teachers College (ASTC), with a regular four-year course for a Bachelor of Arts in education. Fern Johnson described life at ASTC for a typical coed.

✦   ✦   ✦

I never had any other [desire but to] be a teacher. My mother had been a teacher. I thought it would have been nice to go to some of the church schools, but they were all out of state and too expensive. We paid $26.50 a month for board and room [at ASTC], and that was very hard for the parents to scrape up.

We all took agriculture [in addition to our regular classes], and everybody had a garden and we had to keep records on this farm, all the animals, and the crops because possibly you would teach in some little farm school where you would need to know everything. Every girl that went through took agriculture. It was enjoyable to a lot of us.

There was not too much time to study. Our days were quite busy. Working in our garden and going down to the farm to check it and then having to get in bed by 10:30. Sometimes somebody held a candle around.

We didn't come home very often. You just couldn't go home on weekends. We needed those weekends at the library. You had your history, you had your geography and your math, just like we had already had only harder.

[There were] about five women to every man. We had sororities and the Y. I always liked the Y.

And I was on some teams [that] played after school. That was my favorite. Some of us took woodshop and you were trying to prepare to be an all-around teacher wherever you went.

[I did my practice teaching at] an all-Mexican school. It was right down there at 8th and Mill. They would [also] take us in buses way out into the country to "Yaqui town" [Guadalupe]. [All the] students [were Yaqui Indians] out there. A man and his wife were the head of the small school. They had a little lunch program and we did that. We did practice teaching the whole second year. [Also] I was in a training school on the campus.

Quite a few of [the girls] worked. They [came] down from the mining towns. There were people who worked in the dining hall and the business people worked in the offices. They tried to give jobs to the bunch who needed [them]. I [never] tried to get a job because my folks could furnish me with the $26.50 a month.

[All] our clothes were very simple. You took good care of

them. You tried to be neat and have your shoes shined. The dormitories and dining room were kept [clean] by the girls.[59]

❖   ❖   ❖

Many students struggled to get their educations and some, like Irene King, worked right to the end:

❖   ❖   ❖

In 1936, my senior year out at ASTC, you stood in line to ask the dean to let you in on credit; then you had to pay your registration fee before the end of that semester. I was coming up for graduation not knowing how I was going to get it paid. My brother was working and going to school, and he was graduating, too. He didn't have enough to help me. I know I had my graduation invitation and graduation pictures to pay for. Black women could do housework. You got $1 a day and bus fare. I got off the bus from working [one] morning and started through the campus and heard a person [say] they had [a] notice from the office to come and do some work to pay for tuition. I went straight over to Old Main to the office and asked them if they had any work. They said, "No, we don't have anything except housecleaning." So, [during] my final examination, I scrubbed woodwork and stopped and went and took the exam, came back and worked some more, and when the time came I had paid it out.[60]

❖   ❖   ❖

Girls who grew up into young women in Arizona from the late nineteenth through the early twentieth century did not have formal health and sex education in schools. A girl's family, especially her mother, was supposed to educate her about her changing body, her proper role, and what constituted ladylike behavior. Whereas some Arizona Indians celebrated a girl's transition into womanhood, most Anglo and Hispanic girls were unprepared for the onset of their menses and were untutored about sex and sexuality.

When Cecelia Sneezy began her menses, she expected to have

a traditional Apache Sunrise Dance, a long and intricate ceremony that involved having a trained older woman of the tribe for a godmother to lead the days-long dancing. But Cecelia's grandmother could not afford the gifts and food that traditionally accompanied the celebration. Although her grandmother's first husband offered to pay for the ceremony, Cecelia's grandmother declined his offer. Nevertheless, Cecelia's entrance into womanhood was noted by her family.[61]

In stark contrast, and representing a relatively common experience, Exie Zieser remembered hiding her menstruation for two years from her family. Utterly untaught, she had no idea what was happening when her menses began:

♦   ♦   ♦

I just took rags and I'd wash them down in the cellar where nobody could see me and put them back on half wet. It was [real scary]. I didn't know what was happening to me. I didn't know. My mother finally found a rag I'd used [and] came in and told me about it.

It's a wonder I didn't get all kinds of infections because I was scared to say anything for fear they'd think I'd done something I shouldn't have done because we were warned about making boys keep their hands off and all that stuff. When mother and daddy told me to do something I did, [even] if it killed me. [I] never questioned.[62]

♦   ♦   ♦

Many mothers had a hard time talking intimately with their daughters about sex and sexuality. Edna Phelps was typical when she reported that her mother "avoided it," though she did tell her about menstruation before her menses began. Edna was 25 before she knew about sexual intercourse.[63] Elsie McAlister's brother decided she deserved to know about sex from more than the "little book" her mother had bought to give her because her mother did not feel she could talk to Elsie about the subject. Elsie remembered, "He had his wife talk to me face-to-face. I have always been very thankful for what she did. Because she enlightened me a great deal [about] what I was to expect in marriage."[64]

Representing an extreme reluctance to discuss sex with her daughter, Lupe Hernandez's mother refused to tell her about having babies when Lupe was already married and pregnant. Lupe did not know how babies were born until she gave birth to her first child:

♦   ♦   ♦

I didn't know [about having babies]. They kept us completely in the dark. I didn't know when I was going to have my first child. "Well, excuse me," I said to [my mother], "How is this baby going to be born? How? Tell me how?" I was very desperate since I was really in bad shape. "How and from where?" I didn't know, until my mother told me, "Wait my daughter, be patient." That's all she told me. Until the baby was born. Then I knew how babies are born. Can you believe it? I didn't know how babies were born. I was innocent, immature. [She told me] nothing [about menstruation]. I learned little by little with time.[65]

♦   ♦   ♦

Mothers and fathers were more likely to instruct their daughters in proper roles and ladylike behavior than sex and sexuality. But sometimes the two issues overlapped. Irma West and her sisters learned from their mother "not to make ourselves forward [with] men. She'd say, 'Keep yourself straight and clean and don't be too inviting and no one will ever take advantage of you. Be careful and humble, and you will come out safe and clean. Above all things, even to death itself, don't lose your virginity, your chastity.' We knew what she meant. She didn't have to tell us."[66]

Some girls rebelled against contemporary notions of ladylike behavior. Edna Phelps recalled her mother asking her why she could not "act like a lady" instead of arguing with her brothers. Edna believed, "I was indoctrinated that women act differently from men and that my brother had more freedom than I did."[67] Mae Wills remembered: "I was in trouble with my dad all the time, because I much preferred to play baseball with the boys or going coasting or something. He was always telling me it wasn't ladylike, but he didn't do anything about it and my mother let a lot of that go. I know my dad would have liked to [have] made me an old-fashioned lady, [but it] really didn't work with me."[68]

Smoking was new, "flapperesque" behavior for young women in Arizona in the late twenties and early thirties. Benita Fennemore learned to smoke when she was a student at the University of Arizona, but she hid the fact from her mother. She recounted the story of the first time she smoked in her mother's presence:

✦   ✦   ✦

At a party out in Glendale, they were passing some cigarettes and as they approached [me] my mother said, "Benita smokes." So I hadn't deceived her at all. You didn't deceive my mother. So I took the cigarette thinking, "Well, it was now or never," and I'm telling you I was in agony. It seemed to me it was six inches long instead of normal size. I thought it would never burn down. I tapped it and tapped it, I flicked off the ashes thinking, "I'm going to get rid of this thing." I was miserable. Because I knew that my mother was not approving of ladies smoking.[69]

✦   ✦   ✦

Young Hispanic women were formally chaperoned by family members when they went out with young men. Ruby Estrada's mother often escorted her. A widow at 35 who ran her family's hardware store, Mrs. Lopez never remarried, nor went out with a male escort, but she chaperoned her daughters when they dated. "We didn't do what [mother] didn't want us to do. A girl had a boyfriend, he had to come and court her at her home. If they went to the movies, the parents would go with them. They had to be chaperoned. What else [could] we do?"[70]

With such strict family supervision, the possibility of leaving home to go to school opened up vast horizons. Ruby vividly recalled: "Going off to school, you thought you were free. Your mother wasn't around. Your relatives weren't there to spy on you. At home they were always spying on you and you couldn't do anything. My grandfather would tell mother [anything I did]."[71]

Many young women, even with access to advanced schooling,

however, did not feel they had a lot of options for a new world. Fern Johnson recollected her mother's instructions to her and what she felt was before her as a young woman, an educated teacher, and a farmer's wife:

✦   ✦   ✦

Mother talked a lot about a woman's honor and what a good woman should be and what she should learn so that she could do a good job at whatever she was going to do. Families were families, and there were women and there were men and you just did what you had to do. You didn't have too many choices. You know if you're married and on a farm, then you were a farmer's wife, and from then on *you did what the day brought*. You didn't have time to think very much of, "What I would like to do? Where in this world could I go and see?" You didn't go too far from your home. Nothing like now. You know, I never heard, "Who am I?" It wasn't, "What do I do?" It was put in front of you.[72]

DOING WHAT THE DAY
BROUGHT

◆

*When I was alone I said to myself, "I'm going
to buy a little house. . . . I'm not going to go
begging."*   Lupe Hernandez

Whether or not they were full-time homemakers, most women's
adult lives centered on their family responsibilities. Running their
homes, caring for their children, and helping their husbands were
the center of married women's lives. Single women also often had
family responsibilities as adults, caring for parents and nieces and
nephews. Further, some single women had partners with whom
they bought houses, planned trips, and arranged their retirements.

For many of the women interviewed, Arizona remained a
mostly pioneer environment well into their adult lives. That
meant their early adult experiences were not initially significantly
different from their mothers' lives on hardscrabble desert farms
and ranches. Town women had access to the technological
changes sweeping America well before rural women, and that
had an impact on courtship, homemaking, family planning, and
birthing practices. Child rearing, however, seemed similar for almost all the women. In both rural areas and towns, raising children was hard work, often a source of joy, sometimes of sorrow,
and always women's responsibility.

By the time of the interviews, there were few differences between the daily lives of town and rural women. Rural electrifi-

cation, easy access to cars and roads, television, and regional medical centers changed women's lives and made the old rural and town differences much less significant.

The overwhelming majority of the women interviewed married and most never entertained the idea that they would do anything else. While individuals' expectations about marriage might differ, in general, women believed that marriage was their life's work. A few women exhibited the changes open to women in the early twentieth century by postponing marriage until well into their thirties, and some knew they never wanted to marry and remained happily single and self-supporting all of their lives.

Most of the women were young adults in the Depression, and that historical event had an impact on their lives whether they were married or single. Money was tight; farm prices were devastatingly low; and young couples often had to postpone their marriages or delay acquiring things they would otherwise have expected to buy.

Also tracing a more general twentieth-century change, several women experienced a divorce in their lives. For some women, divorce represented a release from an unhappy, in some cases abusive, marriage, and they welcomed the relief. For others, it was a difficult and almost shameful event, but one which they nevertheless carried out.

Several women also were widowed, one of them three times. Like divorced women and single women, widows had to support themselves. In addition, though, most widows also had children to support. Even when they had previously been in extremely traditional homemaker roles, however, most seemed to find the strength to strike out on their own and keep their families together.

Women remembered their courting as young country girls revolving around family outings, such as picnics, country dances, and church activities. Always in groups, with a real community around them, couples courted relatively publicly in early rural Arizona. Elsie Dunn recalls:

✦   ✦   ✦

[I met my husband] at a country dance. People all gathered into one person's home, or maybe the schoolhouse. [We'd] get a couple of musicians and everybody would come and bring the children. [We'd] dance all night. It was about all we had and [it] was all I knew; I hadn't been around any city. [My courtship] wasn't too much. We went to church Sunday and Sunday night, to church parties maybe once a week, and there was a dance maybe once a week. That was it. I don't think I ever saw a show until I was 17 years old. On the 4th of July we used to have picnics. All the people would congregate in the meadows, in the shade. Some of the men would ride into town and bring out a wagonload of ice, then we would make great big pitchers of lemonade. There was anything to eat you wanted, and all the people in the neighborhood were there.[1]

❖   ❖   ❖

Irma West recounted the rollicking scene of her first kiss:

❖   ❖   ❖

We were standing there by the gatepost and he sang a little song that we sang in our program, "I wonder who's kissing her now and I wonder who's showing her how." I liked the boys, but no one ever got close to me. They'd kiss all the rest of the girls but not me. [My sister] told Karl that Irma's going to be 16, and she hasn't been kissed. He said, "I'm gonna kiss her." She said, "Karl's gonna kiss you." "Oh, no, he isn't." I looked up the street, and I saw Karl and about five or six other boys walking down the street from the church; and I couldn't run to the barn; I couldn't go to the lake; I couldn't go any other place. What shall I do? If I go out of the house, they'll see me; so I went back in the little back bedroom in the corner and got under the bed. I heard Karl ask Aunt Belle, "Is Irma here?" "Well, I think she is." She'd heard what was going on, I guess. He said, "Well, can I find her?" "Well, yes, I guess so." He came in and it wasn't very long before the whole family and those boys were in that bedroom, and under the bed he came. That's how I got my first kiss.[2]

❖   ❖   ❖

Town girls went on picnics and forays into the desert, like their country cousins, but from town they went in groups with other young people, rather than with their families and communities. In large towns like Phoenix and Globe young people went to dance halls, cafes, and movies, the newest and most exciting entry into courting in Arizona. Elsie McAlister of Globe explained her courting and exhibited the trust her parents placed in their well-brought-up daughter and her friends:

❖   ❖   ❖

As far as courtship was concerned, we went to the movies. We went to the dances. Went on picnics, always in a group. Occasionally we would go to Phoenix for something special, and if we stayed all night, the girls stayed to themselves and the boys to themselves, too. We [went] up to Pleasant Valley and hiked around and stayed all night, [with a] campfire. We sang around the campfire, talked, and what not.[3]

❖   ❖   ❖

And Edna Brazill told of courting in Phoenix:

❖   ❖   ❖

On Sunday we would go to the desert and have picnics [in] a little open board [wagon] that everybody [would] use, and we would take a party out. When the theatres were open and the road shows would come, we would go. I would go to nearly every movie; and the Rose Tree was a little dancing place downtown, and we would go there and dance. There was no drinking, of course, because it was during Prohibition. Alcoholic beverages just didn't enter into our life then.[4]

❖   ❖   ❖

Showing how nebulous the line was between rural and town life, Irene Bishop remembered:

❖   ❖   ❖

Every place we went was [with a] horse and buggy. A friend of ours had a car and once in a while, as a real special treat, we would take the horse and buggy to town and leave it at my uncle's livery stable, which was on 2nd Street and Mill Avenue [in Tempe]. And then this friend and my husband's sister would pick us up in the car and we would go to road shows at the old coliseum in Phoenix, because we didn't have anything like that at that time in Tempe. We would go by automobile and come back to Tempe, get the horse and buggy, and go home. All the time we were going together, we just had a horse and buggy.[5]

✦ ✦ ✦

There were ethnic and class differences in courting, as well as town and rural differences. Young Hispanic women were strictly chaperoned and held to a rigid code of behavior with young men. Some young American Indian women made marriages that were formally arranged by their parents or grandparents and in which there was virtually no courting at all. Further, some upwardly mobile middle-class couples extended courting, especially during the Depression, to enable themselves to begin their marriage established in their professions with a house and nice furnishings.

Ruby Estrada was always chaperoned to every public function she attended and she recounted: "If you had a boyfriend, he should court you at home, not out in the street. Morals were very different. If you did [talk to boys on the street], you thought you were doing something wrong. It was nothing really, but in your mind. Grandmother didn't want the girls talking to boys on the street."[6]

When Cecelia Sneezy was sixteen, her grandmother arranged her marriage to a young man from a neighboring Apache tribe. Cecelia met her husband in her grandmother's tepee immediately before the ceremony:

✦ ✦ ✦

I just don't want to get married, but I would do it. Because I do according to the traditional way. I didn't want to disappoint [my grandmother] because she raised me and I obey her. So I did [marry]. [I met him] at the marriage. [His grandmother said] you have to go to their parents' place and meet the man, but my grandma said, "No, you can't go there, you have to stay here with me." And I did and this man came to me. I still lived in the tepee [with my grandmother and my husband]. I didn't know that man, but I still had to marry him.[7]

♦   ♦   ♦

The man Mary Moeur married saw her on the street when she was fourteen and decided then and there he was going to marry her. He was at the University of Arizona and she was in grammar school.

♦   ♦   ♦

He was driving Grandpa Moeur someplace, and he saw me going down the street; and I had a beautiful red coat with a black plush trim to it and a little red hat on; and John said, "Dad, see that little red bird going down the street? I'm going to marry her some time."

I finished high school in Tempe and then went down to Tucson to the university. The first year I was down there, John came home from medical school for Christmas. Just as he got off the train, he says to dad, "Dad, I'm not going back unless Mary marries me and goes back," and he had one of his tantrums right there. Of course he was going to finish medical school, but he wanted to marry [me] at Christmastime. Then we went back east, and he finished at the University of Illinois Medical School.[8]

♦   ♦   ♦

Benita Fennemore met her husband when she was a freshman and he a senior in high school. A friend of his little sister, she and Dick did not begin to date until he had finished his undergraduate and law degrees at Stanford and she had graduated from the University of Arizona with a teaching degree. They decided to marry relatively early in their courtship, but,

♦   ♦   ♦

we went together three years because this was the Depression. My third year of teaching I think I had worked up to $150 a month, and Dick was getting about the same in the law firm. We saved our money. First he saved his money to buy my engagement ring and later my wedding ring. While I was buying the lot, he was saving his money to use as a down payment on a house. We used to spend a lot of evenings at his house or my house around the dining room table drawing house plans. Then Dick paid an architect [to] finalize the house plan, and we built our own house. We let the contract just before we were married. His family went to Europe that summer, and we lived in their house while ours was being built. I think we knew every brick put into that house, because every night we'd go out to see what they had done on the house that day.[9]

✦ ✦ ✦

When it came to deciding whom to marry, some young women had a hard time, while others knew without question. Different suitors had various good points and the choice in the end often came down to family and religious values. Clara Kimball, a fun-loving young Mormon woman, was torn between two suitors:

✦ ✦ ✦

My mother said that she liked both of these fellows very much. But, she kind of thought [Gordon] was maybe a little more religious than the other, and she thought the other was a better provider. My father [and one of my brothers] settled on the other fellow, because [they] thought he could have more of a home than Gordon could. [I chose Gordon.] When we got married, we never were rich or anything; but Gordon always had enough for us to live on.[10]

✦ ✦ ✦

Falling in love with Gordon Kimball caused Clara to reflect on her mother's experience in a plural marriage, which she had previously taken for granted. Well into her parents' marriage, Clara's father married his wife's sister, Morilla Gardner, and proceeded to have five children with her. When "Aunt Morilla" died in childbirth, Clara's mother raised her sister's five children along with her own ten. Clara asked her mother about her plural marriage:

✦ ✦ ✦

"I don't see how you could ever go in for polygamy. I guess I don't understand it, but I can't see where a woman could share her love for her husband with another woman." And [mother] said, "Well, if you had to do it like we did [you just did it]," but she said, "I'll say right now (and she said it in a low voice) many times I've wept in my pillow over this. I cried myself to sleep about somebody else sharing my husband." That's all she had to say. [Still] I couldn't ever see why women would do such a thing. I guess in some places, there weren't very many men and so they just decided that some of the women would share their husbands. The authorities would talk them into it.

It wasn't all joy and love all the time. I know that it was an awful hard thing for my mother. I would see it on her face, and I would see her go off if anyone would get on this touchy spot. She would always leave the group and go off and cry about it. And that's as far as it went with our family.[11]

✦ ✦ ✦

Typical of most of the women, Irene Bishop assumed that she would marry and believed she would make sure that her husband had good financial prospects. Also typically, fate intervened, and financial success, in the depths of the Depression, gave way to the desire to marry regardless.

✦ ✦ ✦

When I got married, I just took it for granted it was for life. I had to make the best of it regardless of what happened. We had hard times. We had some awfully hard times during the Depression.

Before I met my husband I was going to marry a millionaire because I knew how hard my mother had worked and what hard years she had. And I wasn't going to have to work. But I turned around and married a farmer, and I've worked hard all my life until just the last few years. So we don't always do what we think.[12]

✦   ✦   ✦

Brenda Meckler married later in her life, partially, at least, because she thought marriage was such an important part of a woman's life. She typified the experience of several women who delayed marriage and supported themselves by working in the professions or business.

✦   ✦   ✦

I had an attitude toward marriage that kept me from taking the step. I just wasn't sure that I was equipped to make a good, strong marriage; and I didn't want a marriage that would fall apart. When I married my late husband, he was someone I had known for many years; and [as] I was older I knew that it could be a good marriage. No one ever guaranteed that, but I guess I was sort of waiting for a guarantee to satisfy myself.

I always approached marriage with the thought that I am taking this on, and I must see that it's a good marriage. I mustn't depend on anyone else, even my husband. This is going to be my job, and he would do his job, and between us we would make it a good marriage. But my responsibility first of all was in myself. I have to know how to make it a good marriage.[13]

✦   ✦   ✦

Some women had no intention of ever marrying. Fern Johnson loved the independence she had as a teacher, but, as she said, "after you go with somebody five years, why you either have to break up [or marry],"[14] so she married. Ruby Estrada reveled in her independence at college and later as a young teacher. "All I wanted was to go to school and teach. I had no thought of getting married. When I left my hometown, I never thought I'd fall in love with anybody. In fact, I think I didn't want to get married. I wanted to be independent. I guess that was what was in my mind."[15] Nevertheless, Ruby also gave up her teaching career to marry her husband, who became a successful attorney.

Representing opposite extremes of the spectrum on romance, Elsie Dunn believed in respect, but not romantic love, while Charlie Daniels reported falling in love at first glance. Elsie Dunn described her husband: "He was a good man, a hard worker; and he worked on a [dairy] farm. He was always nice, gentlemanly, just likable in general. I'm a funny person. I don't think there's any such thing as [romantic] love; only a mother for a child [experiences love]. I had that belief, and I had that all my life. You cared for [your husband] to a degree, and [you had] respect; that's the main thing. I'm funny on that love subject."[16]

By contrast, Charlie Daniels remembered: "I couldn't think [when I saw him walk into the room]. Everything I had been taught vanished! [I had been taught to] know who this person is. Where they are from. Who the parents are. What the parents do. A million and one things I had been taught to ask: Do you have a girlfriend? Are you married? Have you ever been married? I couldn't think of a thing but 'Oh, my goodness—look at this man!' And inside my heart was going. I hoped that he couldn't look at me and tell."[17]

Reflecting on her expectations about marriage, Elizabeth Hovde recalled: "[I dreamed of] the knight on the horse and happily ever after; but I suppose, basically, after it's all said and done, I wanted marriage and a family. I really feel that if women were prepared for marriage, they were the exception rather than the rule. I think 75 percent of us went stumbling through. I often wonder if we helped our daughters any more; but we tried to, and I'm sure our mothers tried to help us far more than they were ever helped."[18]

Weddings in general were simple and home-and-family oriented. None of the women had enormous wedding parties, nor did they go on elaborate honeymoons. Some of the Mormon women went to Salt Lake City to have a wedding in the Temple, but even then, the wedding itself was often small and just the immediate family. Elsie Dunn remembered: "[At the wedding, there was just] the minister and his wife, and little girls were witnesses. We went to the parsonage and had to drive the horse and buggy around in the back to tie them up. We went in the house to the front door, and there was a mad dog. The preacher went out there and killed him before he married us."[19]

Irma West and her fiancé decided to be married at the Mormon Conference. She sewed a trousseau and a fancy wedding dress before they left Arizona. When she and her new husband returned from Salt Lake City and their Temple wedding, they set up housekeeping:

✦   ✦   ✦

He had bought us this little house, and we got a cot and built a straw tic. It was a frame of some material, quite strong, big enough to cover the bed with a hole in the top of it, and we filled that full of straw [changing it every fall,] or else shucks made from corn [which would] last several years. We had a beautiful table that my husband and another fellow had made and he made a little old desk for music, and we had some beautiful tanned, angora sheep rugs.

They covered the living room floor and naturally we had little doilies and pictures on the wall that we thought was very good and we always had something for curtains. But the house hadn't been lined on the inside yet—it was just the boards batted up on the outside—so my husband managed to buy some [real stiff] blue paper that we lined all the rooms inside. [We] fixed up the fireplace so that the snow couldn't get through.

We had a little wood stove with about four little holes on it and a tiny little oven. How in the world I ever cooked on it I didn't know. My husband expected me to bake bread like his mother did in her great big beautiful oven. And I failed and I wondered why.[20]

✦   ✦   ✦

Unlike the Wests, Mae Wills and her new husband moved constantly as her husband traveled the new state working on building roads. They lived in cabins and tents and she loved it: "We really had a lot of fun. We just didn't even know we was having a hard time so we just enjoyed it. You go along with whatever life brings."[21]

Nora McKinney described her life as a farm wife on a ranch in the mountains in the Depression. In many ways, her life was not very different from the generation of farm women before her:

◆　　◆　　◆

I could put up all kinds of fruits and vegetables when we lived on a ranch. I averaged canning six to eight hundred jars of food a year. I had a twenty-five-quart pressure cooker that would hold six jars and we canned all kinds of meat—chicken, turkey, beef, pork. We cured meat, enough to last us a year, and then we sold [the rest]. We would cut up [the hogs] and cure the meat in brine and then smoke it and pack it down in shelled corn. All of the hams and shoulders I covered with newspaper and I would put them in a brown paper grocery bag after they had been smoked and then paste hunks of paper over the brown paper until I had about six layers on it and let it dry. Then I would just wrap it in a mesh or heavy burlap sack and hang it in the smokehouse. We usually packed those things down through the midsummer, and, if we ever had any left over, there was always a big demand for them. Bacon we would wrap in brown paper and then wrap with two or three layers of printed paper and layer [it] in a big box kept in a cool place where it wasn't exposed to the heat. It would rarely form much mold over it, and it was good tasting. We put up an average of maybe one hundred sacks of sausage from the trimmings, and we always put quite a lot of pounded-up chili pepper that we raised that seasoned the sausage. I had a recipe for twenty-five pounds. We hung that [in sacks] and let it dry [in an] ideal size to slice. When it dried, it weighed three pounds and we got a dollar a pound for that during the Depression days. My husband could go to town, and he had certain customers who just had to have two or three sacks of that sausage. You could hang it up on the back porch all winter. It kept beautifully and you would have the nicest sausage, and they liked that high touch of pepper in it. I would always can lots of raw meat and tomatoes and make tamale pies to serve ten or fifteen people. They usually asked me to contribute that when they were having big picnics. I had a big sale of relishes, jellies, and jams for the [local] hospital.[22]

✦   ✦   ✦

Fern Johnson married in 1931 and moved with her new husband to a farm in Peoria. She described her life and the slow progress of technology on the farm:

✦   ✦   ✦

And, of course, there was [the] Depression. But, we didn't go around worrying about things, How terrible; we're in a Depression. That's just the way it was. Now when you look back, we realize what a Depression was.

My mother was sick when she saw [our house]. It had been built in 1919 and they built a cellar and they didn't enforce it and the floor had sunk. It made all the plaster fall off and the windows were broken.

It was bad. Someone just couldn't imagine living in a place like this. So we got carpenters and plasterers and the one screened kitchen they made into a sleeping porch.

We had electricity and we had water [but] we didn't have a bathroom. We kept hoping to have one, but it took all of our money to make our payments on the farm.

The dairy and the farm and the payments always had to come first. There wasn't too much left over to put on the house. It was about twenty years before we finally had a bathroom, two bathrooms then. Somebody said, "How did you keep your children clean?" I said, "I kept my children clean as the families had before." We had the old tub inside the wood stove. My mother had bought us a long one so we were better off than with a round one that you had to wind your legs around. We kept clean always.

We always had enough food because we had chickens. We always had milk and eggs and I baked bread. Food was very cheap to buy. We tried to sell eggs at $.08 a dozen and our cream [but we] hardly got anything for it.

Our children sometimes say now, "I don't know how you ever came through." Many, many people didn't. They lost their places. Even if they didn't, they had to borrow again. I always told our children we always had a roof over our heads and we never went to bed hungry and that is a lot more than some people of my age that lived in towns and had big families.[23]

✦   ✦   ✦

Whereas even poor farm women always had food during the Depression, town women had much earlier access to technological help with homemaking. Electricity came earlier to towns than rural areas, and electric stoves, irons, and washing machines became more readily available. Elizabeth Hovde remembered the work of laundry in her home in Mesa and told the story of buying her first washing machine and inventing a solar water heater:

✦   ✦   ✦

[Laundry] seemed to make the most work. The whole bunch wore white linen trousers, and we'd starch and iron until they were dry or they wouldn't last thirty minutes. Now that was a lot of ironing. It took forty-five minutes sometimes to get those things dry. [Later] I had access to a washing machine at my mother-in-law's, but for the diapers [for] the first baby, it was the hard way on a board, and no water heater.

When our second child was coming along, I just didn't even discuss it. I went in and bought a hot water heater and a washing machine and told them to send it out. I don't think I was annoyed, I was just determined. I had had it. I was very fortunate there too because [when the baby] was just about three months old, war was declared and everything was frozen. Nails, washing machines, everything. You could not buy them. I was just plain lucky or I'd [have] gone through the whole thing again.

My husband was quite good at making things, and we decided there had to be an easier way to heat water; so we fixed a solar heater on top of the roof and piped the water up there. It was just a square box and six feet deep, painted black and the

pipes were painted black also. Window glass on the top and a
storage tank just above the ceiling gave us hot water for six or
seven months of the year. Sometimes, we had to stop and
think. That water is going to turn cold if you don't take
a shower before midnight. But actually it was the first solar
heater that I had ever seen.[24]

✦ ✦ ✦

In Phoenix, Benita Fennemore weathered the Depression as
part of a group of young professional couples.

✦ ✦ ✦

The Depression didn't hurt any of us. There were more young
married couples, and we had good times together. If we had
dinners, they were potluck. Somebody would say, "What are
you having for dinner tonight?" Well I'm going to have this or
I'm going to have something. "Well, let's get together." We
weren't spending money, but we were having nice get-
togethers.

Sundays I remember we had friends here who had set up a
badminton net in their back yard. Somebody would scramble a
dozen eggs and make some toast and jam, and we'd play
badminton. We thought we were having a ball. It brought
people closer together. I don't think the Depression hurt us,
but we did have to plan and [work] together.

There was no air conditioning, so they would build a dance
floor in someone's orange grove and they'd have chairs and
tables about the size of bridge tables out under the trees and
we'd dance on this platform. Ordinarily there would be some
kind of a breeze and it was very pleasant. Of course, there
were movies and parties and lots of double dating. We used to
swim in the canals quite a bit. And also there were a few
[public] pools. [We had picnics] and oftentimes we would have
steak fries in the evenings.[25]

✦ ✦ ✦

Pregnancy and childbirth were natural events for women brought up on farms in rural Arizona. Often attended by midwives, mothers, neighbors, and husbands, as well as doctors, childbirth was in some ways a social event, not as privatized as it would become later in the century.[26] Typical of these women, Clara Kimball told of her first pregnancy and birth:

✦ ✦ ✦

I didn't make so much of [my first pregnancy] like the girls do now. I wasn't very careful. I was so lively. I just ran around. I even got on the plow. I would stand on one side of it while Gordon was riding a horse, and I was about five months along then. She was born in 1911. Gordon had to get in his father's buggy and go up to Safford and get the doctor, and Aunt Rhoda was an old nurse; and she came and stayed right there with me while the doctor was there. The baby was born right there in that little room.

The doctor came right [to] the home. [The baby] had to be turned over and it was quite a process. The doctor brought his nurse, and they worked with me all night long. They took me outdoors for a while to walk up and down the steps to see if that wouldn't help me turn the baby. It didn't come. They just finally worked and worked, she had to be turned so much. Finally she was born.[27]

✦ ✦ ✦

Hospital births were common in mining towns with company hospitals, for some Indian women treated by the Indian Health Service, and for many town women. They were often perceived as more difficult than home births, and there was a general prescription that the women could not leave their beds for at least ten days, which all the women remarked made them weak and unable to cope initially when they returned home. Midway between home births and hospital births, some town women had the alternative of maternity homes run by midwives. They were quite popular, as they were more "professional" than home births, but were not as alienating as hospital births, since they were run in a home and had only maternity patients.

Ironically, even women who had hospital deliveries attended

by doctors had little prenatal care and rarely any information about contraception after the birth. Sallie Lewis, a Mohave Indian, had her babies in an Indian Health Service hospital, but had no prenatal preparation and was terrified about the process of giving birth, as were the other women in the hospital.[28] She "didn't know" about birth control and as she explained about her pregnancies:

✦   ✦   ✦

I don't think I gave too much thought about it other than to feel bad at the beginning and then just took it as a matter of course. That's the way it is.

I don't know how [my husband] felt. He never said. I think most Indians don't express themselves as to how we feel about certain things, especially in that area.[29]

✦   ✦   ✦

Cecelia Sneezy had her first child in 1939 and her last in 1959, a twenty-year fertility span. She had her first at home, her next four at the reservation hospital, and her last three at the Phoenix Indian Hospital. Cecelia's grandmother was a midwife and healer who delivered babies around the reservation and who earned from five to ten dollars a delivery. Cecelia described her first birth with her grandmother in attendance:

✦   ✦   ✦

My grandmother, she is the one that take care of me. I didn't go to hospital. We got snow at that time and she used to be like a doctor or nurse. They would call her and she would go out. I was sick for four months. Then I get my first baby.

[My first child] was born in a tepee without a floor. I was sick, but [my grandmother] didn't take me to the hospital. I guess you know how the old people [traditional Apache] are. She says she is going to make me better. She made a tea [out of] rose bushes that will help me, she said, and I drink it.

My grandma was the one that take care of the baby for me, to help me, 'cause it was my first child.[30]

✦   ✦   ✦

In the more isolated areas, women sometimes called on neighbors to help when the doctor or midwife was unavailable or on the way. Nora McKinney recounted the first time she helped a neighbor: "I had read enough and I had had two children. I knew how to take care of them, so they sent for the doctor at Prescott. He came and said that there wasn't anything that I hadn't done. I left the umbilical cord a little too long, because the baby was maybe ten hours old by the time the doctor got there. He had to come with a wagon and team because there wasn't any train coming down at that time close to us. He said I did all right delivering that baby. I took the baby and went in and greased him good and then bathed him. She nurse[d] it and it lived."[31]

Some women's groups involved in expanding prenatal information for women and others, forerunners of Planned Parenthood, even discussed family planning in a general way. Some women practiced birth control and planned their children. Edna Brazill had a planned pregnancy after eight years of marriage, and she had good prenatal care, part of it from her women's club. She remembered discussing when to have their first baby with her husband.

✦   ✦   ✦

We thought it over and wanted to be established and know just what our future was. We were both old enough and planned our lives that way. I said she was a planned child.

I went to Dr. Salk because I was having morning sickness, in fact all day, and he did give me a shot for that.

I was careful of my diet after I was able to hold food. It was a good thing because all I wanted during those first three months was cold eggnog. So, I got my milk that way. [Later], I didn't drink milk because I didn't think it agreed with me. A nutritionist who was talking out at the women's club one day said, "Oh, Edna, drink lots of milk. You need that calcium." I drank milk after that, but there was about a month or so there that I didn't have any milk.[32]

✦   ✦   ✦

Women discussed birth control with each other, as one woman said, "over a cup of tea."[33] They would share information and discuss methods. Benita Fennemore and her friends all wanted to limit their families. She learned about women's fertility cycle:

◆   ◆   ◆

I was pretty darn careful. We did discuss [the rhythm method] and we tried to follow that as closely as we could.

I can't remember frankly that we specifically planned a certain number. Our main goal was we wanted a family because we both like kids. We never set a special goal except within our limit of what we could afford.

But in those days we didn't discuss it quite as frankly as people do now. I suppose that maybe Dick and I were more intelligent than some only because of our background and education. Of course we used contraceptives. My husband always referred to them as rubbers. He took care of that. He went to the drugstore and he bought them. And after intercourse I would take a douche which was just a matter of cleanliness, as much as a preventative.[34]

◆   ◆   ◆

Several women discussed various drugstore medicines that could be used as contraceptives or perhaps abortifacients. Some rarely used them because they were irritating and "very potent."[35] Edna Phelps was well informed about contraceptive techniques when she married in her early thirties:

◆   ◆   ◆

At the time of marriage, I was armed with a diaphragm and foam because [that had been] my method. I used this when I could.

One time, my period was late and [my husband] was very much concerned, and so was I. He said, "Oh well, we can fix that up." He went to a druggist and got some sort of pill and had me swallow the vile things. I think they had lead in them,

I don't know. They made me awful sick. I did start to men-
struate, but I don't think it was due to the pills.[36]

✦   ✦   ✦

As women talked about contraception, they also discussed
abortion, though it was clearly an illicit activity. Mae Wills recalled:

✦   ✦   ✦

I knew about [abortion], but that sort of thing was hush-hush
because you had to know which doctors did it. I do know at
one time there was this lady here in Globe that did them. I
mean not like the doctors did. I don't know what her method
was, knitting needles, I think. But, you've heard about those
things.

I don't know too much about it because all you did was hear
about it through other women. That so and so is doing that.
There's someone down here that's doing it, and I think most
women wouldn't feel it was very safe to go to her. I don't
know who she had for customers because I'm afraid if anyone
had anything like that done they kept it very quiet. I guess you
could have got in trouble for it.[37]

✦   ✦   ✦

The women who had children all spoke very positively about
the joys and pleasures their children gave them. Child rearing
was almost always women's responsibility, and all the women accepted that as completely normal and natural. Because many
married in the late twenties and the thirties, most of the women
were raising children during the Depression, which added real
financial worries to the omnipresent burdens of early child rearing. Nevertheless, all of the women, when reflecting on their
lives, believed raising their children was their life's most important and rewarding work.

Fern Johnson recalled what it was like on their farm when the
children were little:

✦   ✦   ✦

[Diapers] were a chore. I usually would have a girl come and help me a couple of times a week, and I always used cloth diapers. We'd put them on a tree and hose them good and sometimes boil them in a big tub.

We just couldn't wash every day like mothers do now. I really only could wash a couple of times a week. I'd rinse the diapers out and have plenty.

All five of us slept in one screen bedroom, a double bed, a single child's bed, and two baby beds. There wasn't much room. When grandmother came, she slept here in the dining room with her furniture, and sometimes an aunt would stay on the davenport.

Sometimes [when the children were little] we did then bring a child in to this bed and keep a fire. As soon as they were a little bigger, why we put them on the front porch, a bed on each end, one for the boys and one for the girls. I put up some curtains and some dressers and when it was cold we'd roll down the canvas. It was awfully cold and windy. Sometimes I'd go out and put a little muffler around their head, because we naturally had no heat out there. But we seldom had a cold. We were fortunate in doctor bills. We carried no insurance.[38]

✦   ✦   ✦

Mae Wills remembered being at odds with the older generation over her care of her infant:

✦   ✦   ✦

It was hot, you know what July and August is, and I would put [the baby] in his basket with nothing but his [naval] band and diaper. I would put a netting over his basket and set it out in the shade of the house. I'm sure my mother and mother-in-law both thought that he would die, because they believed in babies having a shirt and a flannel petticoat and a dress and booties. I couldn't stand that many clothes and I didn't see how the baby could. We disagreed on that but then I was away from them; I could do [what I wanted].

I carried him down to the store with me one day with just

the diaper and a little dress on—no hat, no shoes—and I think every old lady in [Ashfork] whether I knew them or not was telling me, "You may not see it now, but that baby will have trouble later on. You're going to kill him. No booties, no cap, nothing." They all thought he should be bundled.[39]

✦   ✦   ✦

Before aspirin for fevers, antibiotics for bacterial infections, and polio vaccine, mothers routinely had to deal with serious, and sometimes terrifying, childhood illnesses. Mothers often had to have their houses publicly quarantined when their children had measles, chicken pox, whooping cough, or scarlet fever. Several women had at least one child die, and others had to deal with chronically ill children whose illnesses exhausted the parents as well as the child. Polio was a special horror of childhood and epidemics swept Arizona, as well as the country as a whole.

Elsie Dunn told of caring for her chronically ill son:

✦   ✦   ✦

He was sick most of the time. I don't know all he didn't have. It was day and night. Sometimes he had croup, he almost choked to death. He worried me so much; I was afraid of losing him.

[My husband] would sit up all night with me all the time. I would be so worn out I could hardly stay up.

He had pneumonia about every winter. I stayed up with him so many, many nights that finally I got so that I would put a kitchen chair in the bed, put pillows and quilts around it, then I would lie there beside him.

I laid there beside him for months on end. He finally got able then to get better. He got able to get out, do a few chores, and finally to work. [He died] ten years ago.

I didn't want any more [children] because I had so much trouble with him. [He was] all I could take care of.[40]

✦   ✦   ✦

Exie Zieser remembered the pain and terror of her son's polio attack, made worse by her experience with the doctor and the hospital:

✦   ✦   ✦

[My] youngest boy had polio when he was in the third grade. He came home from school complaining about his legs hurting. He just fell in his daddy's arms and was crying and my mother was over here eating dinner. Mom goes in and she rubs his legs. She rubbed and rubbed and he just kept crying. I gave him aspirin and he still kept crying. When bedtime came I told the older boy to move in with his daddy in the front room. I pulled the [boys'] beds right close together and lay there and I rubbed that kid all night long. First thing in the morning I called the doctor [who] came and said, "You know as well as I do what's wrong with that child." I said I was afraid, and he said, "He's got polio, definitely. What have you been doing?" I told him and he said, "You've crippled your child for life. You should never rub him, never. You never rub a child with polio." Well, you can imagine how I felt. He said, "Get him down to the hospital as quick as possible." We got him down there, and they wouldn't even put him in a room until we got the money to take down to pay them for it. They had him sitting out in the hallway all that time. Then they thought it was catching, so they put him out in a little cottage in the back. I pleaded with them to put him near the window so I could see him, because they wouldn't let us go in and see him. They did that and a week or more he didn't care whether we came or [not], he was just so out. The doctor told us, "I've got a new medicine that might help this child." And, that was our only chance. He gave it to him and a little girl at the same time, tried it out on the two of them. We didn't think we had any choice in the matter because he told me I'd crippled him by rubbing him. I've found out since that that's the best thing to do [to] keep the circulation going.

He came out of it okay. I'll tell you that was a fearful week. The happiest day of my life was that day that [he] turned and looked at us and talked to us and started crying when we left

him, the happiest day of my life. I came home and cried. After
the doctor told me I crippled him, it just scared me to death. I
think that's the only time I saw my husband cry.[41]

✦   ✦   ✦

Several women took responsibility for children who were not
their own. Generally, the children were orphaned nephews and
nieces, but sometimes their parents had simply fallen on hard
times and the children were rescued by their parents' sisters. Several widows raised children in addition to their own, and Loretto
Coles, who remained single, took on a great deal of the financial
responsibility for eleven nephews and nieces when her sister was
widowed and her brother died. Her help allowed the children of
both families to finish high school and attend college.

Exemplary of these women, Lupe Hernandez had five children, two of whom died. She was widowed when her three remaining children were young. Her mother-in-law then died,
leaving four children, younger brothers and sisters of her dead
husband. Lupe took them into her home. When her sister died,
she also brought in her two nieces and raised all six orphans with
her own children. She never questioned her responsibility to any
of the nine children, although she sometimes wondered if she
would make it:

✦   ✦   ✦

[When people asked], "What are you going to do now?" I also
thought: "Oh, Lord. What am I going to do? With so many
babies."

God helped me, to give me strength in order to lead the
family. God helped me. Me cooking beans, cooking tortillas,
cooking what I could so they had something to eat. God helped
me. Nobody could have helped me if it hadn't been for God.
Because that's one thing I've had faith all of my life. Because I
know that without God we're nothing. We are nothing more
than a leaf blown around by the wind. But keeping God in our
hearts, you know God helps us with so many things. Only
God. And then when things get hard: "Thank you Lord,
infinitely, because You have helped me." And I have a faith in

Him that I will never lose. I will never lose it. Like I say without Him we are nothing, we are, like I say, like a leaf in the wind.

When [the children] celebrate Father's Day, they celebrate for me too, because I was the father and mother. I have a place in both places, on Mother's Day and Father's Day, too.[42]

✦   ✦   ✦

Having raised their children, most of the women talked about how hard it was to see them leave. For some, it was the first; for others it repeated itself with each child; and for still others it was the baby leaving home; but missing their children and dealing with the loneliness was a common theme for nearly all of the women. Fern Johnson recalled: "[Your first child leaving] is the loneliest feeling. My mother told me [after I left], 'I felt like you had died.' I'd never been gone very much, when I went to [school in] Tempe. Same way with my daughter. She would come in and sit on the stool and we talked and we miss[ed] that."[43]

In contrast, Clara Kimball said, "I felt all right about [my children leaving] until my last one left and then I just wept. I couldn't stand the last one going because she was my baby and so close to me." Like the other women, once she got used to her children being gone, she was fine and as she explained: "I had more time. I didn't have anything to keep me home, so I taught music. I had as many as twenty-five or thirty-five children come to my home and take piano lessons."[44]

Children leaving home were only some of the stresses women faced in their married lives. Some women had unhappy marriages which they terminated by divorce. Of the four women who divorced their husbands, all but one were teachers and could support themselves. That one stayed married much longer than she wanted because she had a sickly child and did not believe she could support herself and her child as a single woman. She divorced when her son was twenty-one.

Edna Phelps recounted her short marriage:

✦   ✦   ✦

I am a person who needs a great deal of privacy. He was a person who couldn't stand to have his partner ever shut away from him. If I wanted to take a snooze and go in in the afternoon and shut the door, or if I wanted to sit at the sewing machine and the door was closed, he'd throw it open and say, "What are you doing in here?" This sort of thing.

He had this grandiose idea that when I had this job with Central Arizona Light and Power I would bring home my paycheck and give it to him and he would use it to develop a little real estate he had.

He was a financial failure always. The houses were never paid for, the taxes were always delinquent, everything was in arrears. This is so in violation of everything that I had been reared to believe and the way I practice. It was just different ideals all through. It's ridiculous that I had gone with him for ten years, and he had been arguing with me those ten years to marry him, but I didn't realize that these things were so important to me or that they would be so violated in this relationship.

[I married because of] peer pressure. Every one of my friends at that age were already married, having children. Not that I wanted to be married and have children, but it was the thing to do. He was the most persistent thing in the world.[45]

✦   ✦   ✦

Tillie Garten married in her thirties for one unhappy year:

✦   ✦   ✦

He got drunk at his [own] wedding, and then I was scared of him. We came together again and we had disagreements.

He was drinking all the time. He ran away and wanted to come back; I wouldn't have him. That was that.

I really wasn't deeply attached to him, and I decided I wasn't going to live that way the rest of my life. It takes courage, but I ended it.

I was still teaching. My life was just the same, except that I awakened then. I was in another world. I really was very idealistic, a dreamer. I enjoyed my work, and I went traveling. I had a good life.[46]

◆   ◆   ◆

Three women interviewed were single all their lives and had very different feelings about that. Additionally, many women were single for the majority of their adult lives, either because they married very late in their lives, married very briefly and divorced, or because they were widowed early and chose not to remarry. Many women specifically discussed the possibilities they had for remarriage that they turned down to remain single.

One of the single women, Loretto Coles, believed she had missed a great deal by never marrying, yet she also had offers of marriage she did not accept:

◆   ◆   ◆

I was very interested in business once I got into it and also into my own family. I did go with men quite a bit, but girls and boys weren't living together and they weren't doing all the things they're doing today.

I think a lot of people were always trying to get me married off. And sometimes I regret very much that I didn't get married. I don't say I was just overwhelmed with offers but I could have been married had I wanted to be. But I was really too dedicated to business and family. I wish [my family'd] kicked me out of the nest, instead of me staying there, [but] girls didn't think of living out of the home at that particular time. I think you do feel sometimes like the third wheel on the bicycle when you're single. I feel it more now that I'm older because women outlive men a lot and there's so many more women than men now that you aren't included in a lot of things because it overbalances, too many women and too few men.

I regret that I don't have children, but I have a lot of wonderful nieces and nephews and I'm very fond of them. I think maybe I was almost spoiled by having a wealth of children, but they're never quite like your own, if you come right down to it.[47]

◆   ◆   ◆

Winona Montgomery, on the other hand, was a happily single woman. She never felt any pressure to marry and she supported herself well as a teacher. Active in civic affairs, she loved her life:

✦   ✦   ✦

I built my own house in 1929 while I was teaching. I had a great deal of kids, at school, and I was fond of [them].

I traveled every summer somewhere. I've been in every state in the United States at least once and some of them several times, and Mexico, and I spent a summer in South America, and a summer in Egypt and Africa down through the parks and I don't know how many trips I've made to Europe. I've gone around the world but it's been quite awhile—when I was younger.

We usually left the day school was out and came back about the day it opened.[48]

✦   ✦   ✦

Women who were widowed also lived, at least for awhile, as single adult women, but there were obvious differences between them and women who were single by choice. First, they had to deal with grieving the loss of their husband, and then they had to worry about how they were going to support themselves. Often they had children to support as well. There was a difference among women who were widowed, too. Being widowed as a relatively young woman, especially with children, was a terrible blow and quite unlike the sadness, but acceptance, that older women experienced when their husbands died at a more expected time of life. Many widows, as several of the women who divorced, remarried.

In 1919, when Violet Irving was eighteen and a new mother with a premature baby in an incubator, she was widowed. As she explained:

✦   ✦   ✦

He died just a couple of months [after the Armistice] with flu and pneumonia; a very young, healthy young man, but he died.

[I was] terribl[y] confus[ed]. What do I do? And what do I

do with a tiny baby? When I could take her home I was frightened to death of her. If she'd been a normal baby I suppose I would have taken it in my stride, but I was frightened. Fortunately, my grandmother was still there and she was the one that dragged me through and I went back to work. I had to have someone take care of her. I had to pay for that and make a living for a tiny baby and myself, which I did, until she was between six and seven years old, when I married Mr. Warren.[49]

✦   ✦   ✦

Violet and her husband, who was a businessman, were married for fifteen years when he died in 1938. Although by the time she was interviewed, she had been married and widowed for the third time, she remembered her second husband's death as the most difficult:

✦   ✦   ✦

[There was] so much responsibility, right in the middle of the Depression and the grief of losing my husband [with] one kid in the university and one still in grammar school, and not knowing what in the world I was going to do with the business, because he ran his business right up to the day he died practically.

I [had] kept the books, but I did not have the responsibility of the merchandising and the meetings. We had lost everything we owned, practically, and [I] had to pay debts and bring it back to something worthwhile. It was rough; it was hard, and I wasn't a kid anymore.[50]

✦   ✦   ✦

Mary Moeur's husband, who was a doctor, was chronically ill throughout their marriage. As his illness progressed, she had to take over more and more of the running of the household and their financial interests. She believed her husband's death was very hard on their twelve-year-old son John, who "idolized" his father, but it was not so hard on her:

✦   ✦   ✦

I'd had to be responsible for the home and all for so long because John had been ill, there was really no adjustment. He had been away for months and months at a time at different hospitals.

I never [considered remarrying]. I have had so many dependents, my mother and [my niece] Penny and John, and I thought, "No, thank you."[51]

✦   ✦   ✦

When Mary Moeur was widowed as a relatively young woman, she had no financial difficulties, but when Lupe Hernandez was widowed, although two of her children were grown, she still had children to raise—ultimately nine—and no money. Nevertheless, on the wages she earned in various below-minimum-wage domestic jobs, she saved enough to buy the house she and her husband had always rented, and she fixed it up with her own hard work and that of her grown children.

✦   ✦   ✦

When I was alone I said to myself, "I'm going to buy a little house. Why should I go around moving everything? With God's help, I'm going to build a little house and I am not going to go begging." Here is where I stayed and here I am.

A young woman bought the corner and told me: "Lupe, I'll sell you the house." And I bought it. I paid the pesos. I worked to be able to get this place. [It was run-down.]

When it rained, the water came in and there was no covering. The little old lady that [had] lived there walked around in the water barefoot because it was a lake inside.

I worked a lot on the house. I put up [screen] doors because it didn't have any [and] in the afternoons the ceiling was black with flies. "I'm not standing for that," I told my sons-in-law.

I cleaned a whole lot. Then this girl saw the house was changing little by little and she wanted to take it back. She came to fight with me about it. "You want it back? You pay me what I've put into it. Now it has doors; I cleaned it all up.

Now everything is different. You pay me what I have put into it and I'll let you have it."

[At that time] I was cleaning [a lawyer's] office. I told [him] about what had happened. "Oh no," he told me, "she can't take it from you. She has to pay whatever you ask for it. Take this paper and put it on the wall where she can see it." And I put the paper where he told me. She came and read it and never came back.

Now that the house was mine, we started to fix it up. The inside of the house was very pretty, we put up walls out of cardboard. The house looked very different, really nice. But water would come in from different places. With time, my sons-in-law saw that it wasn't right that I was living in that house the way it was. One of them told me: "I'll knock down the house, I'll build a new one." "Don't do anything for me. You'll leave me in the street?" "No, look, while we build the house, you come live with us." And that's what I did.

Between all of them soon they had the house built. I mixed the cement when I came home from work.

That sidewalk over there, I made it myself. There used to be a puddle there and I made it to walk on and not get all dirty.

By myself in the afternoons in a wheelbarrow I would start mixing cement. And those stairs there in front, I made those too.[52]

✦   ✦   ✦

Family life focused most women's adult lives, but it was not their sole concern. Rather it was the platform from which some went out to work and all went into their communities to shape the future of Arizona and build institutions that would make life better for its citizens.

Edna Porch (Brazill). The picture was sent with her application for a teaching position in Phoenix, Arizona, 1918.

Edna Brazill at her home in Phoenix, Arizona, January 1982.

Pioneer members (prior to 1935) of the Arizona Federation of Women's Clubs. Edna Brazill seated behind the table, third from the right, *in light dress and bonnet, Phoenix, 1966.*

Elizabeth Jessop and Oscar S. Hovde, wedding picture, Phoenix, Arizona, April 1, 1934.

Irma Hansen and Karl West, wedding picture, Salt Lake City, Utah, October 7, 1915.

Irma West in Mesa, Arizona, 1976.

The Phelps' homestead at 12th Street and the Arizona Canal, Phoenix, ca. 1915. Left to right, *Wilmina, Irene, Louis, J. Ernest, and Edna Phelps, on the horse.*

Edna Phelps teaching a Spanish class at the Sunnyslope Senior Center, March 1982. Photo taken by Suzanne Starr, Scottsdale Daily Progress.

The Phelps' family swimming hole. Their property corner was on the Arizona Canal. This is how the Phelps kids made it through the summer. Phoenix, ca. 1915. Left to right, Louis, Edna, and Irene in water; Wilmina and J. Ernest Phelps on bank.

Loretto Coles and friends at Bright Angel Trail, Grand Canyon, May 1, 1942. Coles is third from the bottom.

Loretto Coles's parents at Bright Angel Trail, Grand Canyon, October 18, 1914. From top, Howard Sterling, Maude Sterling, Frank Coles, and Jane Coles; *the guide is standing. Photo by Kolb Bros.*

Loretto Coles in backyard of her home in Phoenix, Arizona, January 1982.

Volunteer Red Cross workers during World War II, Phoenix, Arizona. Loretto Coles, top row, far right.

Mary Moeur in backyard of her home in Tempe, Arizona, September, 1981.

Mary Carter (Moeur) and friends at Papago Park, Phoenix, Arizona, ca. 1917–1918.
Left to right, *Vyvyan Moeur, Mary Carter (Moeur), and Jessie Belle Moeur.*

Fern Foltz and fiancé Raymond Johnson at Dreamy Draw, Phoenix, Arizona, 1930.

Four generations of women, left to right, *Evelyn Fern Johnson Riggs (25 years old), Fern Foltz Johnson (53 years old), Tamara Lyn Riggs (1 year old), and Mary Martha Pore Foltz (82 years old) in Spring 1961.*

Fern Johnson and infant son, Raymond Ray Johnson, Peoria, Arizona, June 1932.

Fern Foltz (Johnson), upper right corner, *and her second grade class. Madison School, Phoenix, Arizona, 1929.*

Clara Kimball at her home in Mesa, Arizona, September 1981.

*Clara Curtis Kimball with her
daughter Olive in Tucson, Arizona,
1912.*

Irene McClellan (King), graduation picture from Arizona State Teachers' College, 1936.

Irene King outside her home in Phoenix, Arizona, March 1982.

Elsie McAlister in front of her china cabinet in her home in Globe, Arizona, August 1, 1981.

Mae Wills in the squash garden at her home in Ice House Canyon, Globe, Arizona, August 1, 1981.

Jane Wilson Drees at her place of business—Wilson Paint and Floors—Miami, Arizona, September 1981.

Nora McKinney with her sewing machine used for her leather work, Globe, Arizona, August 1, 1981.

Brenda Meckler at her home in Phoenix, Arizona, March 1982. Photo taken by Suzanne Starr, Scottsdale Daily Progress.

Exie Ridgeway and Nicholas Zieser, wedding day, September 2, 1928, Phoenix, Arizona.

Sallie Lewis at her home in Scottsdale, Arizona, September 1981.

Elsie Dunn in the garden of her niece's home, Phoenix, Arizona, September 1981.

Winona Montgomery at her home in Phoenix, Arizona, October 1981.

Tillie Garten painting in the backyard of her home in Tempe, Arizona, September 1981.

Madge Copeland at her home in Phoenix, Arizona, March 1982. Photo taken by Suzanne Starr, Scottsdale Daily Progress.

Cecelia Sneezy at the Globe Arts Center, Globe, Arizona, October 25, 1986.

Ruby Lopez Estrada's mother, Mercedes Garcia Lopez, and her younger sister, Josephine Lopez, in their hardware store in Sonora, Arizona, 1929. Ruby often worked in the store with her mother after her father died.

Ruby Lopez (Estrada) as a teenager standing in front of Brophy Preparatory School, Phoenix, Arizona, 1931.

Ruby Lopez Estrada's grandparents, José and Josefa Garcia and her mother, Mercedes, in Globe, Arizona, 1890.

Ruby Lopez Estrada in her home in Phoenix, Arizona, February 5, 1991.

BUILDING ARIZONA'S
COMMUNITIES

✦

The happiest women I've known are the ones
who have given to others.   Edna Brazill

The impulse to begin working on community projects often
came from women's traditional roles of nurturing their families,
promoting religious values, and being good neighbors, but the
work itself pushed many women far beyond their original ideas
of what they were capable of doing and what was possible for
their communities. Arizona women were intimately involved in
building the institutions that made their communities better
places to live, and they were responsible for initiating social and
cultural facilities, such as schools, libraries, parks, hospitals,
churches, and museums, as well as programs that substantially
improved the health and welfare of Arizona citizens. They were
also extensively involved in traditional party politics. While town
women were often more able to be involved in extensive club
work than rural women, all of the women belonged to at least
one organization and most to many more.

Women used many avenues for their involvement. Some
helped people entirely on their own, but more often women
worked in women's clubs. Some women's clubs were primarily
for the social pleasure of the members, while others were dedicated to solving particular problems, building specific institu-

tions, and promoting the community. Women's clubs were often highly class bound and sometimes defined a woman's position in the community, just as a man's occupation defined his position.

Based in American notions of the importance of voluntarism, women's clubs did community development efficiently, creatively, and joyously. Many women found lifelong fulfillment in their club work and women's clubs, which often had their own buildings, gave women their first public, physical space to join together for both pleasure and community development. Through their clubs, women negotiated an entrée into the public sphere that did not interfere with their self-definition as homemakers, yet allowed them to build institutions that changed the public nature of their communities. Sometimes denigrated as centers for women to gossip and fritter away time, women's clubs tackled social problems and built community institutions before local and state government became involved. Ultimately, once the programs were established, government or private corporations often took them over.

Women also worked with men in voluntary organizations to improve the community. For instance, women served on public boards for community schools and were intensely involved in work for political parties in Arizona. Women were leaders in the movement to integrate Arizona schools and public places, sometimes working alone and sometimes with organizations such as the National Association for the Advancement of Colored People.[1] All of these volunteer efforts changed the face of Arizona and made it a better place to live.

Women became involved in community work for many different reasons—the desire to meet people, the will to help out, the need to further family goals—but overwhelmingly women claimed that altruism made them happy: "I think as a whole, women do want to help others, and if they don't, when they come into their sunset years, I don't think they're nearly as happy as they are when they really feel that they have been a help to humanity in general. The happiest women I've known are the ones who have given to others."[2]

Furthering her husband's career and expanding her friendships led Benita Fennemore into extensive volunteer work in Phoenix:

✦   ✦   ✦

I think some [women] actually liked an outlet from the routine of home life. When I got involved, it was for my husband to promote his status and we became known. That's really why I got into things, because I could do so much to help him. He said it was important in law to make contacts in the community, [because] lawyers can't advertise.

He said, "I don't resent anything you do in the community and all I ask is that you participate in the community things that you enjoy, but don't neglect the children. I never want my child[ren] coming home from school and not find[ing] their mother home, but the more you can do, [the more you will] help me." That was really the beginning. Instead of playing bridge, I got involved in community activities and I gained a great deal, because I think it's very personally rewarding—no money involved at all, but just public-minded citizens. I think I've been fortunate. It's rewarding any way you look at it.[3]

✦   ✦   ✦

Sometimes volunteer work led into paid work. Edna Brazill jokingly explained why she took a job at Luke Air Force Base after she and her husband closed their family business: "I have been working just as hard all these years with volunteer service, and I decided I'd like to work for something and get paid for it."[4]

Several women discussed ways in which they helped others as individuals from their sense of what a neighbor does: "I was right in the middle of everything. Any job that there was for women, I was right there. I'd go into homes and take care of sick people. I had to dress a person to get ready for burial. Somebody told me how to do it and I did it. When it came time for anyone to be buried, I generally had to take part in trimming the caskets and helping to make the clothes. And that was about all the community work there was to be done, tak[ing] care of each other."[5]

Madge Copeland routinely brought baskets of food to shut-ins and helped elderly neighbors in her Black South Phoenix neighborhood: "Church, community and any political field, I'll be active as I can because I have a personal missionary project that I have of my own. I'm not depending on any organized missionary group, but I have my own missionary obligation."[6]

All seemed to agree with Irene Bishop who said, "I think [community work] gives you quite an inner peace."[7]

Women worked in service organizations that spanned the spectrum of community concerns and demanded extraordinary commitment. Mary Moeur recalled that she "never worked that hard at home in my whole life" as she did working on sales for the Goodwill.[8] Jane Drees detailed the extensive involvement she had on boards for state-funded schools:

✦   ✦   ✦

I have always been active in community work. I served on the board for the school for the deaf and the blind in Tucson for two years, and I was on the board for the Arizona Community College for eight years. My husband was very agreeable to taking the time to do that and never presented any opposition to that sort of activity.

The responsibilities with the Arizona Community College board were greater than that for the school for the deaf and blind, [which] was more an administrative, policy-making sort of thing. We decided on budgetary procedures and amounts and we observed the regulations of the school and made recommendations for changes. For the Community College board we had budgetary responsibilities, policy and program responsibilities. We had to determine and approve building programs, particularly the campuses that were just starting, and the relationship between the state board and the governing boards in the districts. Altogether, it was very challenging.[9]

✦   ✦   ✦

Community projects often expanded and even transcended the boundaries of women's traditional concerns. Edna Phelps was active in the Sunnyslope Citizens Council, which was built on earlier women-dominated councils, and which developed a park and community center in her neighborhood.[10] Fern Johnson became an expert on water issues, which she pursued through her active work in the Farm Bureau.[11] As the widowed owner of a general store in Skull Valley, Violet Irving led an extensive campaign to bring electricity to her remote rural area. The process tested her sense of self and showed her intuitive political savvy. In the late 1930s, when the fight began, she had minimal access to electricity for her store because she had a gas-powered generator: "We had coal oil lamps and we had enough [generator produced] electricity much of the time to run a refrigerator and freezing cabinet for our meat because the store had a meat market and lights, but you didn't overload those things . . . the meat came first."[12]

She was anxious to have regular access to electric power and was delighted when electricity was extended to Kirkland, seven miles from Skull Valley. On the basis of a survey, however, the company decided that there was not enough demand in Skull Valley to extend the service. Irving and others "scouted around in that Valley and subscribed enough to pay for the line and had a contractor that would build it. Just about that time the war broke out and everything like that was frozen. [It] was over for the duration."[13]

At the end of the war, Arizona Public Service (APS) took over the local power company and again decided not to extend power to Skull Valley. Irving and others came up with a scheme to attain power under the auspices of the Rural Electrification Act:

◆   ◆   ◆

We joined Verde Valley and a rural electrification deal. The power company wasn't pleased, because we were over two mountains from the Verde Valley, but we figured by double forces, we'd do better. It was up to us to get subscribers: $5.00 apiece and their name and what they would use rural electrification [for]. We were accepted.

The power company started fighting us because they didn't want rural electrification, and whether they knew it or not we didn't want rural electrification either, because we would have had to form the board and run the darn thing and I couldn't see myself doing something like that. But we stayed with it right to the hilt.[14]

♦   ♦   ♦

By signing up everyone—ranchers, miners, and people way out in the "boondocks" who "never had a hope of getting power"—the organizers built a powerful coalition. APS capitulated and extended power to Skull Valley in 1948. "[I was the leader in the electrification movement from] let's call it necessity. I had the one business there that really [needed it]. By that time there were frozen foods and that meant a lot to my business. It was a necessity as far as I was concerned. Naturally, it was up to me to accept the biggest part of the responsibility, because I was the one who was going to benefit the most."[15]

During World War II women did a variety of home-front volunteer work. Benita Fennemore helped the wives of servicemen: "I got involved with Traveler's Aid. There were so many wives trying to follow their husbands, and they would arrive here and maybe they had run out of money. Traveler's Aid would advise them and contact their families, and you name it. From that I got very involved on the YWCA Board because the two sort of identified with each other. These wives would have to have housing and we'd take them back home or send them on or contact their families. They were just heartbroken wives and sweethearts that were following the troops across the country."[16]

Marjorie Mandel was a Gray Lady during the war. She took a Red Cross course to work with wounded soldiers and ran the canteen for troop trains in Florence. She also worked at the POW camp with Italians and Germans. She and the other women would talk to them in the little German they knew, which ironically in Mandel's case came from her knowledge of Yiddish. The women would "just be with [POW's]. We didn't bring them any food, but we did write cards for them. We amused them in some way or another—the girl who could sing would sing and those who could play would play."[17]

As a young, single working woman, Loretto Coles worked nights and weekends for the Red Cross under the auspices of the Junior Chamber of Commerce.

✦   ✦   ✦

I was in the Red Cross Auxiliary [and worked] at the canteen. People donated a lot of grapefruit. We had grapefruit juice, we made sandwiches, and donuts and we did not have an automatic donut machine. We had to roll the dough with our arms. The canteen was set up very modestly. All of a sudden a troop train would come in with two hundred boys. We were never allowed to know in advance. But we had to be ready to serve them. We had coffee and donuts and grapefruit juice. We had thousands of comic books that people in Phoenix donated, and we also had cigarettes. The boys used to throw mail out of the windows and we would mail it for them.

The trains that weren't allowed to stop, we would take a cold drink or something and pass it through the windows [to the boys]. Many of those trains were on their way to California [where the boys would go] overseas.

I happened to be organizer of Saturday's and Sunday's group, and I was chairman of the working girls.

Women worked four hours, and if it was at night, the police picked them up at their homes and delivered them back.

We chairmen never thought of being afraid of crime or anything. I drove down to the railroad tracks at 2:00 in the morning. If we ran out of food, we had to get it. We were usually well stocked, but you never knew when the trains were coming. We would have to go to a dairy, maybe. Here we were driving around all hours of the night and it never dawned on me to be afraid.

I don't think the boys needed the food or anything; it was a morale builder. [They] just loved it when they came in, the soldier boys.

Many of [the Red Cross] women still meet on their particular days if they're alive, but my group, being younger [and working women], scattered to the winds once the war was over.

I must say that was quite a rewarding period in my life. The more volunteer work you get into, the more you feel capable of.[18]

✦   ✦   ✦

All of the women were involved in women's clubs. Some were affiliated with national women's groups, such as the General Federation of Women's Clubs, Delta Sigma Theta, and the Young Women's Christian Association (YWCA); some were religiously affiliated, such as the Council of Jewish Women and various missionary groups; and some were professional organizations, such as the Altrusa Club and the American Association of University Women (AAUW).

Edna Brazill described the Glendale Women's Club, which was typical in its combination of self-improvement and service:

✦   ✦   ✦

The Glendale Women's Club was founded in 1901 by a group of women and called the Glendale Culture Club. Women's clubs in those days were interested in culture, education, and reading. In 1902, it was federated with the General Federation.

Their main objective in the community was [starting] the library. They built the building, so we had benefits [to pay for it], and it was quite a social club, too. We always had a welfare department which did a tremendous amount of work among unfortunate girls. I started the Girl Reserves [which the Women's Club] carried on through the years.

Once a month in addition to our regular meetings with the book review, we did Red Cross work. We did all those drives. The Glendale Women's Club [would] sponsor anything.

We've accomplished a lot during the years. Our women were always ready to help. It's been such a joy to me. I've seen the progress year-to-year, and the old and the young together. There's no generation gap there.[19]

✦   ✦   ✦

Delta Theta Sigma, another women's service and social club with a national affiliation, was one of Irene King's primary outlets. She explained:

✦   ✦   ✦

Delta Sigma Theta is a Black sorority [that is] very active in advancing all types of activities in the community. This year we worked with the Help Center and put on this program through the health clinics and hospitals [to give] complete examinations to people.

We take an active part in scholarships to keep a student at ASU. We give at least eight eighth graders $25 to buy books. We take part in the United Fund.

We go in for educational and cultural [projects]. So many girls who are Deltas are outstanding in their community. That's the difference between typical sororities and this sorority. This sorority was set up to help provide opportunities for Black women.[20]

✦   ✦   ✦

Several women were involved with the YWCA at various times in their lives. The YWCA had an active chapter at Tempe Normal and organized entertainment for young people in mining towns like Bisbee, Globe, and Miami. The Phoenix YWCA provided programs for young working women and became a model for racial integration in Arizona:

✦   ✦   ✦

The YWCA was early in recognizing the problems related to the Black people. There were many outstanding, capable teachers at Carver High School here and we used to include them in events at the Y and they would come and they were quite accepted by both the staff and the board and the community who attended something at the Y. My own mother was active at the YWCA and she greatly respected some of these teachers from Carver High School. There weren't many places in the community where these teachers could go for social gatherings, but the Y was quite a cross section. They tried to keep it that way, and we [also] had a cross section on the board of different religious faiths.

We were always looking for minority groups to work on the Y. That was the first [Anglo] organization I recall that became oriented to minority groups.

[At the Y, we tried] to find sufficient housing and we had gym classes for health and well being.[21]

✦   ✦   ✦

Economic and social class played a large role in who did volunteer work and what kind of programs were promoted. A certain amount of leisure time was necessary before women could be involved in volunteer work. In organizations like the YWCA, middle-class women sponsored programs for young working-class women, who had only limited resources both in terms of time and money. Exie Zieser was very involved in the Maricopa County Club for the Blind but did no other volunteer work. She explained, "I didn't have time. With a blind husband and working full-time and my kids little, I was just about as busy as I could be without any more social activities."[22]

Compare her experience with someone like Benita Fennemore, who saw her volunteer work as "her" job in her family and who described the immense task of being part of a large capital-fund drive for St. Luke's Hospital. Working on the St. Luke's board was at the top of the social scale in Phoenix—the St. Luke's Ball is still the premier debutante ball of the year—and association with St. Luke's presumed both time and substantial familial monetary involvement. Even though St. Luke's was at the top of the volunteer social scale, it had always depended on women's work since its very origins as a tuberculosis refuge served by Episcopal women doing good works.

Benita Fennemore explained:

✦   ✦   ✦

Since 1942 I've been active at St. Luke's Hospital on the board
of directors. I've been chairman of the board of visitors, I've
been chairman of every function that they have had at different
times for fund raising; and just the other day I was at St.
Luke's Hospital for the opening of their behavioral science
building, and I am thrilled to death with it. It's so challenging
and so marvelous.

It will be a treatment [center] for parents that abuse children,
[and for] alcoholics and drug addicts. There is so very much
that can be done for them if they have a facility where they can
get the treatment, and this new building is equipped with a
beautiful patio and swimming pool.

It is one of the finest institutions west of the Mississippi
River. If you have a spark of human concern about human
beings in this day and age, you can't help but be challenged by
this. The women have already given $1,000,000 to it and we've
pledged to give another million. And we have given it by
having our annual St. Luke's Ball, and we have an annual
fashion show. We're always working on fund-raising for St.
Luke's.[23]

✦   ✦   ✦

In addition to raising money, Loretto Coles and several other
women worked in various hospitals and clinics as volunteers:
"We did a lot of jobs around the hospital. We also worked in the
free outpatient clinic. They had the pregnant day, the diabetic
day, and women could work on any one of those days they
wanted. You were allowed to weigh and get people ready for the
doctor. It was the first time anything like that had been [done]
and it really made news in the paper."[24]

Many women took part in organizing cultural institutions.
Benita Fennemore recalled the noted Phoenix philanthropist
Mrs. Maie Heard inviting women to join the Phoenix Fine Arts
Association, which met in her house: "The nearest thing we had

to an art museum was when the fair came and we had an art exhibit at the fairgrounds. Some of us used to go out and work very hard uncrating paintings and hanging them."²⁵ Out of those humble beginnings, and largely due to the work of this organization, evolved the Phoenix Art Museum.

In much the same entrepreneurial fashion, a group of Tempe women associated with the Tempe Historical Society organized the Tempe Historical Museum dedicated to preserving the city's heritage:

✦　✦　✦

We got to talking and we thought it would be so nice to have a museum in Tempe. They appointed Mrs. Getz, Irene Bishop, Betty Hayden, and me as founders, but so many people helped.

We had our first meeting in Hayden Library. Our goal was to have a museum, and we had meetings about once a month. We knew a building was way off, but a few of us started collecting things. We'd find somebody who had something that they were willing to give.

I don't like taking credit, but I was really a collector of the old-timers. I knew them so well. They'd say, "Mary, we'll let you have it because we've known you and we know you'll take care of things." I've gone out to every old barn in Tempe, Mesa, and Chandler. We've even found old farm machinery out there in the fields.

It's been a lot of work. We'd get down on the floor and we'd scrub and clean and polish and refinish. I wouldn't work like that at home for anything. You couldn't hire me to, but we really did manual labor.

We all had things stored under our beds so there was hardly room under the beds for anything more because there was no place else to store it. When the city put up the new library, they loaned us one big room for the museum, with no partitions, no nothing in it. We thought, how would we ever fill it up? We started bringing our things from home [and acquired the old post office and other things from town. We refinished furniture and re-upholstered] and did different things to raise money.[26]

◆   ◆   ◆

Women joined churches and synagogues to realize their faiths; some even started the churches in their communities. Additionally, all were involved in a broad variety of women's organizations within their various religious groups, most of which had both social and charitable purposes. Fern Johnson recalled: "The women started this church. It was the only church in the whole settlement around [Peoria], and the cowboys came in and women started it in their own homes. Women right away started to organize Ladies Aid and missions. We didn't need social reasons."[27]

Irene Bishop recounted how her Methodist church adapted to the rigors of ranch life and the long distances people had to travel: "When we lived out there in the country, it was hard to always go to the meetings in town at church, so for a couple of years we would divide in circles. Once a month we would have a general meeting. I would go to the general meeting and bring ideas and report to our circle. We [still] try to do whatever we [can] in church, see people [who are] ill and things of that kind."[28]

Shortly after Brenda Meckler arrived in Phoenix in 1918, she recalled:

◆   ◆   ◆

There were a few Jewish families and they gravitated toward one another and they would meet in different homes [to] have social affairs, a dance sometimes in a hall over somebody's store somewhere.

The Council of Jewish Women used their funds to alleviate stress. They had a children's milk fund [which] was one of their major projects—not just [for] Jewish children; it was [for] all children.

At that time there was no structured organization for charitable purposes as there is now. At that time, you heard the term "tzedakah." It's more than just charity; it is good deeds. It is serving others who needed help.[29]

◆   ◆   ◆

Marjorie Mandel remembered the activities of the Council of Jewish Women after World War II:

✦   ✦   ✦

The Council of Jewish Women brought in emigres from Russia or places where they were being oppressed. We tried to get them in and get them settled. Quite a few settled in Phoenix and quite a few went on to relatives in Los Angeles and [other] cities. We had to find them places [to] live, and we had social workers [to] help people who needed help.

Some of the girls were teachers and taught them English and held citizenship classes to [help them] pass the examination. The Council of Jewish Women sponsored a man who was just too poor to open a little business and he became quite a success.

[We raised funds with] raffles and card games and various things and, of course, we did get donations from some of the big people, like the Diamonds.[30]

✦   ✦   ✦

Irma West, a devout Mormon, dedicated herself to community work, almost all of which was centered in church organizations: "I was the president of the Relief Society. I was president of the Mutual Improvement Association. And the primary, for the children. I was vice president, I was secretary, I was chorister, [and] I was a teacher for every class that there was. I think I held every position that was available for a woman."[31]

As a minister's wife, Sallie Lewis was intimately involved in all phases of church work, including Sunday School, summer Bible camp, Bible study, and missionary societies:

✦   ✦   ✦

I was on the board a number of times, helping with programs with all of the Presbyterian churches, in women's work [which] was Bible studies and raising funds for the church and the needy, helping the missions overseas, raising scholarships for students in the ministry of the church, and sewing for hospitals, and our Indian churches.

There was a sense of satisfaction in doing things for people, helping them out, making someone happy or making someone feel relieved about things that were bothering them, and seeing them come to church and participate.[32]

✦   ✦   ✦

Through their children, churches, and schools, many women became active as adults in organizations devoted to children, such as the Boy Scouts, Girl Scouts, Girl Reserves, and Parent Teachers Associations (PTA). Important community resources, these organizations promoted social and community values and sometimes were small islands of integrated activity even when schools were segregated. Marjorie Mandel sponsored a Girl Scout troop in Florence, which had both Anglo and Mexican-American members: "There was absolutely no segregation whatever. That was one town that did not segregate. I, being the only Jewish [woman], would very readily find that out and never did I find anyone who was a bigot. Never."[33]

Edna Brazill organized a Girl Reserves group in 1919. The YWCA's equivalent organization to Girl Scouts and Camp Fire Girls, high school girls joined together for fun and wholesome activities:

✦   ✦   ✦

The YW is the triangle, body, mind, and spirit. And so we tried to bring out all phases of that. Of course, we had games. They played indoor golf, we had teams and we would compete with other schools. In June, the residents of Iron Springs would open up their cabins for the YW to take the Girl Reserves up for a week or ten days, and that was delightful. At Christmastime we had a candlelight ceremony at the Episcopal church in Phoenix. And we would have a weekly meeting. I thought that we were really making leaders out of those young girls and later, it certainly developed that way. Many of them have been president of the Women's Club, and others continued to be active in the YW. We also did service in the community in different ways just as the Girl Scouts and the Campfire Girls and the Y Teens of today.[34]

✦   ✦   ✦

Many women were involved in the Parent Teachers Associations of their children's schools. The groups provided programs to enrich the schools and often bought extra supplies and organized field trips. Elsie Dunn was the president of her PTA as a farm woman, where the PTA was "mostly mothers. [Though] quite a number of fathers also belonged, they didn't attend the meetings too much, because most of them were busy farmers." In the early 1920s when cotton began to be a cash crop in Dunn's area, she recalled being asked by her local state representative to organize the PTA at the new "colored school" in the Fowler District, which was opened for the children of Blacks who had arrived to pick cotton. While in this case the PTA reinforced community segregation, both groups had some interactions through the umbrella of the PTA.[35] By contrast, by the 1970s, Cecelia Sneezy, a San Carlos Apache, was on the education committee of the newly integrated Globe High School and was president of the PTA.[36]

Women who did paid work also were involved in a wide variety of volunteer organizations, some particular to their professions. All of the teachers were members of their district and state teachers associations, and some were very active leaders. The Arizona Teachers Association was integrated, and both Irene King and Winona Montgomery were on the state board. Both worked successfully for a variety of issues, including school lunch programs, pay equity, tenure, and improved benefits, especially health insurance and retirement. Anne Bush and Winona Montgomery were active in the American Association of University Women (AAUW), which often joined with teachers associations, PTA, and women's clubs to further common community goals. Montgomery was instrumental through her AAUW affiliation in lobbying legislators for the re-establishment of kindergartens in the state.[37]

Additionally, some professional women's clubs were based on

male professional clubs. The Altrusa Club was an international professional women's club modeled on the all-male International Rotary Club. Like Rotary, the Altrusa Club existed to promote business public relations and international exchange. Loretto Coles was active in the Phoenix Altrusa Club and described their programs:

✦   ✦   ✦

The Altrusa Club always had a project. The county hospital was way out west [with] a lot of sand and dirt and dust around it. We developed [the land] all around the hospital so there wouldn't be so much dust. In the wards, there were no curtains or partitions between the beds; we had curtains put up.

We also [put] a chair by each patient's bed, which they hadn't had. At Christmas, we had the name of every patient and their age. Instead of [us] exchanging gifts, we [bought gifts] for all the patients in the Maricopa County Hospital. The women would go out there, a tree would be delivered, and they would [give a party].[38]

✦   ✦   ✦

Across the board, Arizona women were involved in party politics. All voted conscientiously, and most echoed Irma West's comment that "I never miss a voting day. I feel that's my privilege."[39] While Irene King purposefully stayed out of politics to avoid conflict,[40] many were enormously active as Democrats and Republicans at all levels of government in the state. They worked as registrars, poll watchers, precinct polling place staff, fund raisers, and they belonged to the women's organizations of each party. Arizona politics were not solely the province of Anglo women either, for Ruby Estrada, Madge Copeland, and Cecelia Sneezy were all active as registrars in the Democratic Party. Sneezy recounted her political work both for the party and her tribe:

✦   ✦   ✦

I started working with Representative Panchi from District 4 to be his politics helper. [The County Democratic Party] wanted to tell the Indian people how to vote. They didn't know. I helped [the Party Chairman] and I registered people. I guess I

registered more people from San Carlos [than anyone] in
Arizona. I campaigned for people for governor, [state senator,
and representative], and others, too. I used to help at the
tribal council and campaign for the chairman. I helped with the
ladies. I go around and tell people I know [who I'm voting
for].[41]

❖   ❖   ❖

The Depression propelled Madge Copeland into politics,
where she ultimately became the first Black appointed to county
government in Arizona.

❖   ❖   ❖

I really launched out into the political field because I saw where
the Democratic Party would help poor people. I knew the
Republicans were always for the rich, and the Democrats really
were down to earth with the poor people, and I worked very
hard on that, in registration, in campaigning, and anything to
help the Democratic Party. I really went into it full force
because I'm always for the underdog.

I started way back in '32, the year President Roosevelt ran.
He just enlightened the whole country, opened up so many
positions that Negroes never would have had. [Government's]
the only way [Negroes] have improved to where they are now.
I have always stuck with the Democrats.[42]

❖   ❖   ❖

Jane Drees held a variety of posts in the Republican Party, including precinct committeeman and county chairman of Gila
County. She capped her volunteer political career by being president of the State Federation of Republican Women.[43]

Edna Phelps was also an active Republican and described her
involvement in developing the party in Maricopa County in the
1950s, but she ultimately became disillusioned with both parties
and became a politically active independent:

❖   ❖   ❖

I became a deputy registrar as well as a precinct committeeman.
In July and August, tremendously hot [months], a number of
us volunteers spent time in a little donated trailer. It was parked
on Dunlap Avenue under paloverde trees. There were no
buildings along there then, and the volunteers sat in there with
the petitions for different Republican candidates and asked all
comers to sign. We were working for Mr. Eisenhower, John
Rhodes, [and] Barry Goldwater, and Maxine Brubaker, a
personal friend of mine, was running for state superintendent
of Public Instruction. She had had two sessions in the
legislature.

We just sort of took it for granted, we were Republicans. It
was the thing to do. By the time I was forty-five and was
talked into becoming a Republican precinct committeeman, I
considered myself a strong Republican. That lasted for about
five years.

Then, as the old farmer said, "I began to read." I realized
that neither party had a stranglehold on the truth or the good
of the nation. They were each striving to put themselves in
power and to retain that power regardless of how it affected the
nation.

Over a period of years, I have had occasion to write to Mr.
Goldwater, to ask him his voting favor. One of them was
when ERA was attempting to have an extension of time. He
wrote me back an abominable letter. He just damnationed me;
he said, "In no way is this constitutional. I will in no way
vote for this. It is a preposterous request, and you can depend
on the fact that I will do everything I can to vote against it."
Well, I thought, I'm ashamed of the day that I ever tried to
send him to the Senate!

So, now my registration is automatically independent and
will remain that way the rest of my life. I will never associate
myself with another political party.[44]

✦   ✦   ✦

Beyond party politics, Madge Copeland worked with the National Association for the Advancement of Colored People (NAACP) to advance economic opportunities for Blacks in Arizona and to integrate public accommodations in Phoenix:

✦   ✦   ✦

The NAACP picketed a lot of places. We picketed Woolworth's and the Rialto Theatre that had all that segregation. [We] first started with the lunch counters. They didn't serve you at all. We just kept that up until it was broken down. As one of the Negro ladies told the head down there at Woolworth's, "We just bought something over here on this side, why can't we buy food?" They couldn't deny it, because after all they were serving customers all over the store, and that was broken down. There was trouble out to the airport. They would not serve Negroes, but that was run by the city. I have a very dear friend and the two of us went down to the mayor's office as soon as it came out in the paper [that] they had refused to serve [a Black] entertainer and his wife. We told [the mayor] the story and we said, "[The airport] is run by the city, and we would like to have it open so that all races can go, because all races are supporting it." He said, "I'll let you know my decision at 5:00 o'clock this afternoon." So we left, and promptly at 5:00 he called, right on the dot of 5:00 and said he had made the change and it would be open [to all]. I said to [my friend], "Let's not hurry. They may put something in the food. Let's wait a little while. They may be so mad they want to make us sick." We had a lot of fun with that.

We were [also] trying to work [in the NAACP] for jobs and to go to these businessmen and ask them to hire [Blacks]. Some couldn't hire them because the girls had never had any training in typing. They were not allowed to go to the business school, and what typing they could do, they learned in high school. We were successful in getting some in the different offices to hire [Blacks] working in the files.[45]

✦   ✦   ✦

Although she was well known in the community, Copeland was harassed for her work and charged that the FBI investigated the Phoenix NAACP during the 1950s, accusing it of Communist associations and implicitly accusing her of Communist leanings. She held firmly: "I don't know anything about Communism—not the first thing. All I wanted for Negroes was to rise out of the horrible condition they were in because they were held down by the white race. I [always] remembered my grandmother's training [when I was harassed. I put] my head straight up in the air and just kept walking."[46]

Women's volunteer work crossed political and ideological boundaries and expanded everyone's ideas of what was possible for Arizona. The work women have done has influenced every major social institution in the state and has made Arizona a better place to live in almost every way. Most of what people believe makes communities livable—churches, schools, parks, libraries, hospitals, museums, theaters—was started here by volunteers, the large majority of whom were women. Driven by their ideas of appropriate activities to help their families and communities, the women built much of what is most cherished in Arizona and also expanded their ideas of what they themselves were capable of doing. Often they went far beyond what were "typical" women's concerns for children and social welfare.

Women's volunteer work was real work that has benefited the Arizona community immeasurably. During this time, however, the majority of the women interviewed also were part of the paid labor force in Arizona. Their work for pay changed over the years as well, and, like their volunteer work, was instrumental in developing the Arizona of today.

WORKING FOR PAY IN A
MAN'S WORLD

◆

I had fifty cents cash the night my husband died.
Madge Copeland

Mirroring their contemporaries around the country, most Arizona women worked for pay for at least part of their lives. All of the women interviewed held paying jobs at one time or another, or worked in family businesses with their parents or spouses. A substantial number worked the majority of their lives, and many were the sole support of themselves and often various family members—aging parents, younger siblings, children, and nieces and nephews.

Most women liked their jobs and many were dedicated workers. Their work lives gave them friends and a place in the larger community. All talked about the ways in which paid work assured them a sense of self-respect and validation. Regardless of whether or not women liked their jobs, however, all of these women worked because they or their families depended on their earnings. They did not work for "pin money"; they worked for the same reasons men work. In all cases, women's work provided a substantial proportion, and sometimes the totality, of the family income.

Women's paid work generally was an extension of women's traditional unpaid work in the home. Although they did a wide variety of jobs, most women worked as domestics, laundresses, cooks, sales clerks (of household goods and clothes), office workers, beauticians, social workers, and teachers. Little changed in types of work available to women until World War II, when factories increased production to meet the demands of war, opening industrial work to women.

Women's paid work also often had a life course to it. Most women worked when they were young, before marriage, some even when they were schoolchildren. Many left the paid labor force after they married, especially when they had young children. However, all the single women worked to support themselves, even when they could have lived at their parental home without working. Often married women with children reentered the paid labor force when their children were older. Additionally, of course, many women who married were propelled back into the work force regardless of their wishes when their husbands became disabled, died, or left. Widowhood was common and divorce increased as the century wore on, making marriage a frail barrier against the necessity of paying work. Further, many women wanted to work even when they were married and their husbands were employed. Especially during the Depression, however, there was substantial opposition to married women working, and many jobs, particularly teaching, were simply closed to married women. Nevertheless, women persevered in their desire to have paid work, took all the opportunities that opened to them, and became an important segment of the Arizona labor force.

As schoolchildren, many women worked on their family farms, ranches, and businesses. Sometimes they were paid and sometimes not, but in all cases, if they had not done the work, someone else would have had to do it and be paid. Through their work, which was often more than simply "chores," they contributed in real ways to the family economy. Clara Kimball did a wide variety of jobs, from working on haying to processing honey for their family ranch in southeastern Arizona. Elsie Dunn also did every form of farm work with her parents as they moved from farm to farm working for themselves, working as farm hands, and sharecropping. When her father died, Ruby Estrada immediately began selling hardware in her family's store. Though neither her mother nor any of the girls had ever worked in public before, after Ruby's father's death, all ran the store and kept the family together.[1] With her farm labor, Edna Phelps brought money into her family, which was struggling to home-stead a new farm in Phoenix:

✦   ✦   ✦

[I first earned] money picking cotton in 1918 when long-staple cotton came to the valley. There was a field just east of the house. Anyone could get a job picking cotton. It paid five cents a pound that year, which was rather good. We'd work all day and maybe get a dollar. One of the men who oversaw the picking crew told me that I was getting too much trash in my cotton. He had told me in the beginning to not only pick the bolls, but [to] get those that had dropped on the ground. I was supposed to shake the dirt out and put them in the bag and I was getting too much trash in mine. Afternoon, we'd weigh our cotton on the supervisor's wagon. He had scales hanging on the back of it. I had eight or ten pounds by noon, and I'd get my little forty or fifty cents, then I'd pick until evening. We did this on the weekends. It was schooltime, and it was neces-sary, of course, that we go to school.[2]

✦   ✦   ✦

Several women began working in high school to help put themselves through teacher training or business school. Eliza-beth Hovde worked for several summers so that she could go to Flagstaff to Northern Arizona Teachers College to study busi-ness. It was during the Depression, and her parents were not able to send her. She could only save enough to have one semester in Flagstaff but was able to go to the University of Arizona for two semesters when her parents moved to Tucson from Morenci. In Tucson she could live at home and attend school. Also during the Depression, Irene King successfully worked her way through her teaching degree at Arizona State Teachers College in Tempe, but she was literally cleaning rooms on campus on her last day of finals to finish paying her tuition.[3]

After they completed their schooling, but before they were married, all of the women did paid work. Even a woman like Benita Fennemore, who never worked again after she married, taught school and proudly supported herself. Some women, like Edna Phelps, Tillie Garten, and Jane Drees, all of whom ultimately married in their thirties, worked in a variety of jobs around the state. Phelps and Garten were teachers, while Drees was a social worker

✦   ✦   ✦

with Traveler's Aid which involved meeting planes and assisting children and elderly people in reaching their destinations, wiring ahead to be sure they would be properly met, and making sure there were provisions along the route for them to be cared for properly. There were so few agencies active in actual welfare work in Phoenix, we were glad to accept federal funds in the old Emergency Relief Program, and we began to help the so-called transients, the cotton pickers and the people who were traveling because they had been driven from the Dust Bowl. We issued relief and made every effort we could. [We helped them to return home or move on to other destinations if they could.] Otherwise we endeavored to settle them and help them develop roots.[4]

✦   ✦   ✦

Farm and ranch women worked alongside their husbands doing a variety of tasks, from bookkeeping to fieldwork to running to town for supplies and equipment. Elizabeth Hovde worked with her husband on their ranch where they grew fruit, cotton, alfalfa, and wheat. She was responsible for doing the accounts and books and buying supplies in town.[5] Fern Johnson fed the calves on their dairy farm and had a thriving business raising chickens, turkeys, and eggs for sale in town.[6] Mary Moeur, whose husband was ill for most of their marriage, worked on their ranch raising cattle and cotton, even though she was originally a town girl from one of Tempe's most prosperous families:

✦   ✦   ✦

[I took care of the farm.] I had these irrigators [who] didn't know about the different fields. I'd be out there with them at midnight showing them how to irrigate, can you imagine?

I owned another small ranch out on Priest and University. John had bought me some dairy cattle, and so I told the help, we've got to get this herd down there because [there] was plenty of forage. They got on their horses and I got on mine and we herded the whole herd of cattle down Broadway. It was a long trip, because the cattle started off in all directions. I thought I could hear a car behind us and I looked back and I saw this big black limousine come along. When it got up beside us, it stopped, and [the driver] said, "My lord, it's Mary Moeur!" It was Dr. Gammage, [president of Arizona State Teachers College], and he said, "Mary, this gentleman's a noted educator from the East and [I] was showing him around." He had just said, "Dr. Gammage, are there any cowgirls left in Arizona?" [And there you were.][7]

✦   ✦   ✦

Irene Bishop and her husband lived on a ranch in Tempe. Anxious to make some money for the family, Bishop began taking in guests, ultimately transforming the working ranch into a guest ranch.

✦   ✦   ✦

We lived on Rural Road for forty years. That's where I ran a guest ranch from about 1930 to 1942, during the Depression. I decided I was going to do something, but our daughter was little and in school. I had taught school, but I thought my hours wouldn't coincide with hers and there would be no one to take care of her when she came home from school. I saw an ad in the paper, along about September, that some lady from New York wanted a place to room and board for the winter in a modern, refined home, and gave the telephone number. She was in a hotel in Phoenix. I called and asked her if she'd be interested in coming out. She came out and looked around, and we took her back and she got her luggage and moved in. That was the beginning of the guest ranch. After she'd been there for about a week, she said, "Why don't you get a second lady. It would make more profit for you and company for me because this is out in the country and there isn't very much to do." I said, "Well, I don't know how I'd get a second person." She said, "Leave that to me." She went to the Chamber of Commerce and told them. In about a week, we had the second lady. We only had one bathroom. We had two bedrooms and a sleeping porch, but just one bath between them. [Our family continued to] use the bathroom for baths, [but] we used [the] outside toilet. We gave up all our modern conveniences and took the second lady, start[ing] the guest house. The next year people [who] wanted to come started calling, so we put in one cottage and still people wanted to come, so we put in a second. Then [my husband] added onto the back of the house. We extended the sleeping porch. We had a large bedroom for ourselves and made a bedroom for our daughter and we [put in] a bath. So it was a little bit more modern.

When I had the [first] two ladies, I did the laundry and the cooking and everything. As it grew, I started having help, and after we had it in full swing, we had always three. [Two] of them had to be married because we had [only] two little places for [help] to live. We had a cowboy, [who] did the yard and rode with the guests; we had a cook and then a girl to do the cleaning of the rooms and wait tables and help in the kitchen. I did all the shopping, supervised and planned all the meals, [took] the guests everyplace, and met planes and trains. The guest ranch was mine and everything was my responsibility. It was quite a job.[8]

◆   ◆   ◆

Town women did a variety of jobs. Domestic work, sewing, office work, clerking, and business were common, as well as teaching, the most typical professional job for women. Like some of the farm women, several women worked with their husbands running family businesses. Irma West ran a cafe with her husband and even learned how to cut up meat. Later she helped her husband run their service stations.[9] Edna Brazill worked twenty-one years in her husband's mortuary until they sold it to her son-in-law.[10] Violet Irving did her husband's books for their store in Skull Valley and then took over the business when he died.[11]

A single woman all of her life, Loretto Coles also worked in a family business. A sales manager and buyer in her father's department store, she described the kind of work she did and also some of the many ways women were employed as service workers in stores:

✦   ✦   ✦

I was manager of the china, glass, silver, and gifts. I had to keep track [of] the market all the time. If we were out of something, it had to be purchased. If you had too much of something, you had to get rid of it. A lot depended on your relationship with the public. People who were merchants were kind of jealous of the lines they held and like[d] to hold them exclusively.

Sales people [were] better in that day. They took great pride in helping customers. They kept a little book. If something came in [that] they remembered Mrs. So-and-So [might like], they would call her. It was on a much more personal basis than it is today [but women clerks were paid very little].

We [also] made drapes [in our store], and we had women that worked in the sewing rooms. They made draperies. They also made slip covers. It was all seamstress work. They were all widows and it was very cheaply paid labor, twenty-five cents an hour.[12]

✦   ✦   ✦

Coles recalled the case of a manager in her father's store who sexually harassed women workers:

✦   ✦   ✦

I had just come into the business and my father had brought a man that he was very fond of from Bisbee, who was the manager.

One day a [sales] girl came to my Dad and she said, "I'm going to sue your firm." Dad said, "What for?" She said that man took me over to that office, and he offered to put her through business school if she would submit to him. Apparently, other women had [been harassed] but this girl was the only [one] who spoke up. Of course, [my father] was flabbergasted. He trusted this man, [who] was a great man with the Presbyterian church here. He sang in the choir; he was well respected by the public. He had a lovely wife and children.

My Dad had [a] meeting with him that night after work. The man had to admit that it was so, so [Dad] took the keys to the store and [the man] had nothing more to do with the business. [Dad] bought out [his] stock in the company. However, you'd be amazed at the public. People closed charge accounts, [but] Dad did not want to harass his family or him. The story that went around Phoenix was that Dad was making room for his children who were out of college and that this man had to go, [which was not true].

Then women who worked up in our sewing room [who were] mostly widows so hard up for money (and [it was] hotter than Hades up there) came to my Dad and said [the ex-manager] had grabbed their bosoms when they went by, snapped their garters, and everything. He was "a feeler"; I don't know that he actually did anything worse. But [the women] were afraid [to] tell on him, because they were afraid of losing their jobs. My Dad was completely unaware.

The minister came to my father [to support the ex-manager] and Dad [told] him [what had happened]. [The minister] said, "I'm sure those women are going through the change of life." He upheld that man to the world's end.[13]

✦   ✦   ✦

As a newly married woman who had supported herself teaching for nearly a decade, Edna Phelps needed a job to help pay the bills because her husband earned little consistent money. School districts refused to hire married women teachers, so she was unable to return to teaching and struck out into the business world, finding a job as a home agent for a local electric company:

✦   ✦   ✦

I finally got a job with the Central Arizona Light and Power, which is now the APS. [It] paid $80 a month, plus $30 a month for car expenses. We were assigned various districts of the city to go out and try to sell equipment to the women that would use added public services—refrigerators, ranges, house lighting. We were obligated to take the La Salle University correspondence course in home lighting before we could qualify for this job. I had the very poorest part of Phoenix. I would go to homes and try to first check their home lighting. In some of the hovels, the home lighting consisted of one bulb suspended from the ceiling, and I was supposed to tell them about the shape of a lamp shade and the color of the lining. I was supposed to tell them that it should be white to reflect and the type of bulb they were to use, when there wasn't money to buy bread.

There were a few new homes going up. A gimmick that the girls used in all seven districts was to spot a subdivision or even a new home that was going in and immediately rush back to headquarters and sign that address up for all the electrical equipment they could think of. They'd sign them up for a range, a refrigerator, home lighting and cooling, and all we had to do when we signed them up was to hand this list to the salesman. It was not our job to sell, it was the salesman's job to go out to that home and sell [the] equipment. We got credit, since we had turned in the prospect.[14]

✦   ✦   ✦

After she divorced her husband, and following another ten years as a high school teacher, Phelps took a job working in her doctor's office in Buckeye in 1949:

✦   ✦   ✦

I worked for about a year and learned the head office and back office stuff, gave shots, did urinalysis and blood tests. The doctor had to drive into Phoenix about once a day because the only hospitals were there, and I was left with some rather serious situations while he was gone, which wore me down. I remember one poor Black woman came in, she'd been stabbed in the side of the neck here and she was bleeding terribly, and all I could think to do was put a dry pressure pack on it and make them get her into Phoenix to a hospital because there was no one to sew her up, and I saw she had to be sewed up. But things like that happened. We did have one doctor on call when he would be gone and that was a doctor in Litchfield. One woman came in [once when the doctor was away], extended in the front, and said, "The doctor told me I was going to have my baby here in the office, and it's due." I thought, "What do I do?" So, I call[ed] this doctor in Litchfield and said, "Come as fast as you can." I got [the woman] as comfortable as I could in the birthing room. Luckily the baby didn't come until [the doctor] got there. I was called to help with the baby and hold a little chloroform over [the mother's] nose while she was going through the worst. Then the doctor handed me the baby and said, "Syringe out the throat." Well, how did I know how to syringe out the throat? I'm a high school teacher. Luckily, both the baby and the mother lived and went home. That job was really an education. I learned a lot.[15]

✦   ✦   ✦

Jane Drees stopped social work when she married at the age of 37. After her father died in 1947, she began to work with her mother in the family paint and glass business in Globe. Following her mother's retirement, Drees took over the store and ran it herself until her brother-in-law joined her in 1965 and expanded the business to include furniture and floor coverings. At the time of the interview at the age of 74, she was still working every day.[16]

In 1929, Madge Copeland was suddenly widowed. She decided to try to open a beauty business for Black women in Phoenix, but she needed training in the new waving techniques:

✦   ✦   ✦

I went down to the Adams Hotel to have special instructions [because] the [beauty] school students were white and they did not want any Negroes. The lady [who] ran the school was French, and she wanted me to have this [training]. She and her husband taught me how to Marcelle wave.

I had no family [in Phoenix]. My husband died in 1929, and I had no relations [here] at all. [I was] left heavily in debt. I didn't have a dime. [I] didn't have anything but just the determination to work and take care of my children and educate them. All I wanted was life, health, and strength. I felt I would come out of it, but I had fifty cents cash the night my husband died.

I had nothing to do but work and manage. If you don't manage then you won't make it. [With] the few dimes I had, I did just that. [My] three children got ten cents a day for lunch, and sometimes that would be all I had. I didn't have another penny. But I got my money every day with the customers, so I worked the beauty business [in my home] up to six operators and myself. Some nights it would be 11:00 or 12:00 before we'd finish. Customers were glad to come here and they'd meet and talk and have fun. I put a music box in and the music would get good and they'd have to stop and dance it off. We enjoyed it very much, I assure you, [for] twenty-five years of service. It did help me to get all of my children educated as far as they would go.

I didn't have over five or six people actually cheat me [during the Depression]. Most of the ladies were working people: they worked out in service, domestic work in the homes of white people.

I had all classes: the sporting class, the alley bats, the working class, and a few women [who] stayed home. The alley bats [lived] a very loose life. The sporting women catered only to the white businessmen downtown. Those women catered to some of the richest and most respected white businessmen [in Phoenix]. [These women] rented little cabins downtown and were very, very smart. Some of them were highly educated and came from California to do that kind of work to pay for a home. [One of them told me,] "I can pay for my home and take care of my mother in two years. I can be through and then I'm through with the life. I'm going back to teaching." We had those who kept up with all the news because they had to discuss current events with these businessmen.

They were all working women who supported me, no matter about the classification. Some of them were very kind to bring clothing that was cast off from the rich people and give me for my children. Some of the high-class sporting [women], if they saw something they thought I wanted [like some fancy rolls or food] they would bring it. It was very thoughtful of them.

I would have some customers at five o'clock [in the morning], especially some of those sporty women who wanted to go to work. They paid extra for it because they want beauty through the day, too, just like at night. They would come early to get all prettied up to go to work, some of them were very beautiful and some very ordinary.

[During World War II] the 364th Infantry moved here and that brought in loads of women, wives and sweethearts. They would give us lots of work, as long as they stayed here. Even after they left, we had enough people to keep three to four beauty operators busy. Mine was the first Negro shop. I was very glad to stay at home to be with my children, and I made home comfortable and happy for them so they'd want to stay here. The other children came here to play. It was open house. We had no keys to the house. I allowed all of the children to come here whenever they wanted as long as they respected the place. Of course, the food went out fast, but I enjoyed it. So this was headquarters. I call it city hall #2.[17]

✦   ✦   ✦

Teaching was the most important job for middle-class women in Arizona. Most women teachers were trained at one of the three institutions of higher education in Arizona, and they were dedicated to their work.

Although teaching was predominantly a woman's profession in Arizona, and though it fit well with having a family and raising children, until World War II, teaching was only for single women or widows in most districts. Elsie McAlister recalled "Marriage Cancels This Contract" stamped in big block letters across the top of her teaching contract each year in Globe, and Benita Fennemore postponed her wedding for two years in order to save enough money to set up housekeeping, since she knew she would be fired once she married.[18] Edna Brazill also delayed her wedding and then secretly eloped:

✦   ✦   ✦

After [World] War I was over, married women could not teach in the Phoenix schools. My husband proposed to me and I said, "No." I was going to teach two years because I want[ed] to save [as much] money [as] I [had] spent on my education [to give to] my mother, if she ever need[ed] it. She never did need it, but I was afraid she would, and that was just understood.

The next summer I got married [anyway] and kept it a secret, so I could teach one more year, and no one knew.[19]

✦   ✦   ✦

Married men had no such restrictions, as Elsie McAlister remarked, "The marriage ban didn't apply to the men. We didn't have equal rights in those days [and inequality] was very much in evidence."[20]

While education and the development of school districts have always been important to Arizonans, teaching jobs were often hard to find for new teachers, especially in desirable areas, such as towns and cities, and salaries were always low. Many women had to begin their teaching careers in small, rural communities where rules for teachers' social conduct were strict, where teachers often had to board with school board members, and the entire community knew exactly what the teacher was doing at all times. Benita Fennemore remembered, "Teachers did not smoke, they didn't drink in public. Teachers were social leaders, especially in smaller communities."[21] Edna Phelps began teaching far away from her home and family in Phoenix:

✦   ✦   ✦

I wanted to get into secondary education because that was my field; so I had to live away from home in Pine, Arizona, a little Mormon town. I had to pay rent and room and board. My salary was $160 a month for nine months and I paid $40 a month for room and board. I had a little room on the corner of this boarded house; it was not made of brick, just up and down boards. Through the cracks, I would see the snow in the winter. There was no bathroom; I'd wade through the snow at night to go to the outside WC. We dined on red beans a great deal, because the only time there would be any fresh meat in Pine [was] when one of the cattlemen butchered and would sell some beef throughout the town. My landlady would buy some and we would have meat, but, otherwise, the menu was very often beans. I wasn't used to quite that much cold in the winter, but I stayed the nine months and taught in all the levels of the school because there were only four teachers. Two for primary and two for high school. I would have to go to primary during the day while one of the primary teachers came over and taught her specialty. The principal filled in where he could with American government and so forth. Those were very mean years; $160 didn't go very far. I did send a good deal of my money home, but deposited [some] in the local bank.

   During my nine months there, I had helped with the young people's beehive [a Mormon church teen youth] group. I had attended their Sunday services and had lived in the home of a returned missionary and his wife and also in the home of the bishop and his wife. I had adapted to the community and

they had even gone so far as to say they were spotting a boyfriend for me, one of the cowboys. [But] I was a little homesick
for the Valley. I wasn't used to the snowy climate, and I was
separated from [my] boyfriend.

[I had] absolutely no social life. When I finally told the
principal I would like to leave, I asked him if he would write
me a letter of recommendation. He pulled out a form that had
"educational preparation," "classroom ability," and other
characteristics [on it]. He checked everything "Excellent,"
except "community relations." He said, "I would like to check
this 'Excellent,' but since you are not a Mormon, I cannot."
So, I was pleased that I got as good a recommendation as I
did.[22]

✦   ✦   ✦

Two years later, Phelps went to Marana to teach:

✦   ✦   ✦

When you're in small high schools, you've got a three-ring
circus. You teach your major, you teach your minor, you teach
anything that you have five hours of credit in. I taught home
economics, I taught Spanish and English and had a couple
of hours during the day with seventh and eighth grade, because
they were with the high school. It was a farming community
and the other teacher who joined the faculty the same year I did
and I seemed to make a hit. We were invited out a great deal
into [people's] homes and wined and dined and accepted. I had
been going steadily with a young man in the community
[whose] mother was the postmistress. The principal was a very
straight-laced man [and] he didn't like this. He wouldn't even
let kids walk down the hall holding hands—they'd be called
into the office for a reprimand. The principal called me into his
office, and he said that my contract would not be renewed
because the community felt that, as steadily as I was going with
this young man, I was married to [him] and they did not hire
married teachers, so I was out.[23]

✦   ✦   ✦

In contrast to Phelps's experiences, Winona Montgomery taught at Phoenix Union High School from 1923 to 1939 and then at North High School from 1939 until she retired in 1963. A single woman, Montgomery taught history and social studies and sponsored myriad activities for students, including plays, the YWCA, Big Sisters, and various school clubs. She "almost never" missed a basketball or football game, and she had lots of friends from her teaching. She was active all over the state in teachers' organizations, and she made sure that women teachers' salaries at Phoenix Union were equivalent to men's, taking on the principal when he attempted to give all the men a raise and none of the women. She traveled every summer, as soon as school was over in May or June, and was usually gone the whole summer with a schoolteacher friend. She believed her travel improved her teaching, and she visited every state in the Union, plus Mexico, Central and South America, Europe (several times) and Egypt and Africa. Teaching was at the center of her definition of self and she loved her work.[24]

Veora Johnson, like Montgomery, is also a single woman whose career as an educator defined her life. Sent to Mesa by the president of her normal school, Johnson arrived in 1927 to begin her life as a teacher. Ultimately becoming the first Black woman to hold administrative credentials in the state and one of the first Black school principals, Johnson spent her life in the Mesa schools, actively pursued her own professional development, and dedicated herself to the education of minority students, even endowing a scholarship for minority high schoolers.

Johnson remembered her early years:

✦　✦　✦

At first I was reluctant [about coming to Mesa] but my [college] president convinced me that I should come because I might be able to motivate and help other Black Americans. Emotionally I left every month when I got the paycheck, but it was so small, [after] I paid the bills, I didn't have the fare back [to Texas], so I had to stay on. [I earned] $90 a month and you could not cash the checks. They became vouchers. There was a man on Main in Mesa who [would cash] the voucher [at a] discount. It started off at 10 percent and later 15 percent. We were just that desperate to have the dollar.

Segregation in Mesa was very interesting. In the beginning there was no segregation at all. Finally, segregation began at the old Webster School, and it was for the Spanish-American only. There were very few Blacks, but as soon as they began to increase in number, then a room was set aside for them over at the old Webster School. These two minority groups were there, not integrated, but there. One occupied one area and one another.[25]

✦   ✦   ✦

Later separate segregated schools were built in Mesa. Mexican-American students were integrated with Anglo students before segregation for Blacks ended with the Arizona Superior Court ruling ending school segregation in Arizona in 1953.[26]

Having worked hard for her degree, Irene King began teaching in an all-Black, segregated school in the Phoenix Elementary School District:

✦   ✦   ✦

I graduated from [ASTC] in 1936 in May and there were no vacancies. A week before school was to start in September, a friend of mine married, and, if you were married, you were automatically [fired], so I got the job that she had.

I began teaching [a special first grade] at Booker T. Washington with fifty-two children [with] an age range from 6 through 12. You kept those slower children in the primary grades until they were old enough to drop out. You did not send them on. If they didn't do the work, you retained them.

You just [had to be] organized. You have a group playing something over here and a group playing something over there. The main thing was to include the little "lost" child, the one who just didn't seem to fit in. How were you going to bring him around to become a member of the class? My principals always asked, "How do you do it? They just sit and laugh and talk all together." I said, "Yes, it takes six months to get everybody laughing and talking with one another." I didn't see any reason why they couldn't talk, as long as they didn't disturb other people. They were free to do that. I told [my principals,] "It takes six months to get them to that point, then you spend the next three months telling them to shut up."[27]

✦　✦　✦

A gifted teacher who loved her work, after her first year at Booker T. Washington, King taught forty years at Dunbar Elementary until her retirement in 1977. She has a scrapbook for every class she ever taught, and she made a substantial impact on her students, many of whom have gone on to become leaders in the Black community in Phoenix.[28]

Charlie Daniels, also a Black teacher, moved to Arizona because she could not find a teaching job in Texas. She worked for the Bureau of Indian Affairs in the early fifties and taught at Fort Apache for two years before she

✦　✦　✦

went to the Pima Reservation because that was only place that had an opening. They were desperate for teachers. They couldn't keep the people, [because] it was so isolated. Sometimes schools are more than one hundred miles apart and in between there is nothing but desert and an occasional tree. The school is all there is. The first place I was working was at the bottom of [a] red clay hill. In the wintertime you did not get out. You had to buy enough food to last from the time the first snow fell. You purchased everything that you need[ed] before the first rain or the first snow. Until it dried up, you were there. The children were captives and the teachers were captives.[29]

✦　✦　✦

Prior to 1940, several teachers, Anglo and Black, were involved in various "Americanization" programs, primarily with Hispanic and Indian students. Fern Johnson began her teaching in 1929. "I was hired at Madison to teach Spanish children. They kept the Mexican children in separate [classrooms] for about the first four years trying to Americanize them."[30] And Elsie Mc-

Alister recounted how students were taught in Globe throughout the thirties:

✦   ✦   ✦

The Mexican children were never discriminated against as far back as I can remember. We had an Americanization room [for] the Spanish speaking children [who] knew no English. It was kind of like kindergarten. They went there the whole year and then they would go right into the first grade and it was a big help. We have nothing like that now. They tried to work with the parents to make them understand that English was necessary for the children if they were to go to our school. I worked quite closely with the Americanization teacher. We started a rhythm band, and we combined her children in the Americanization room with my first grade. It worked beautifully. She worked so marvelously with those children. I wonder sometimes how they learn the English language like they do after they have been in a home that speaks nothing but Spanish, because it was hard enough for me to take two years of Spanish in high school. But they do beautifully. It was the same way when they brought the Indian School children from the reservation to Globe schools here. I said to one of the teachers one time, "How is it that these Indian children do so much better when it comes to learning English, the proper use of nouns and verbs." She said, "Well it's because they don't hear their native language at home [by which the teacher meant English*]." She said, "Our kids go home so many of them to illiterate parents who say, 'I ain't got this and that,' and they just don't learn it like these other children do."[31]

✦   ✦   ✦

*The teacher saw their "native language" as English, when, in fact, the students' native language was Apache, a language that, after all, predated English on this continent. This is one of the many ironies of the "Americanization" movement.

By the 1970s, Globe schools had different programs and phi-
losophies for dealing with Hispanic and Indian students. Com-
mitted to a bilingual multicultural approach, the high school
hired Cecelia Sneezy to work as a counselor with Apache students to help keep them in school and combat the high dropout
rate. Without formal educational training for teaching, Sneezy
worked as a teacher's aide on federal grants. "The first hour I help
[the bilingual teacher] with [Apache] history and the second hour
I go down to the [language] labs. I don't know much about the
lab, but I helped them and talked to them and explained to them
in Apache, our own language." Although at first Sneezy faced
some opposition from teachers who were opposed to teaching
students their Apache heritage in the public schools, Sneezy's
work proved a big help in keeping students in school and raising
their self-esteem.[32]

Arizona women followed these relatively predictable career
paths, taking jobs that were related to their traditional roles, until
the Second World War began. With the war and the tremendous
demand for workers, all kinds of new job opportunities opened
up, some completely unrelated to the kind of work women previously had done. Women who had never worked for pay before
entered the labor force and women who had been doing traditional low-paid "women's work" were able to leave those jobs
and take new, higher paid ones. Further, old strictures against
some women workers were lifted. For instance, nearly every
school district in the state suddenly allowed married women to
teach and even aggressively recruited married women. Clara
Kimball went back to teaching music in Benson, which gave her
much pleasure and a feeling that she was helping the war effort.[33]
Benita Fennemore, who had always had household help, found
the best she could do once the war began was to have a young
woman live in her home and help out around her war job. They
called her "Jenny the Riveter," and she essentially held two positions.[34] Irene Bishop had to close her guest ranch in 1942 because "there were factories for women to work in, and I couldn't
afford to hire help [at what the factories paid]. With what I
charged [my guests], I couldn't afford to pay the help. They all

went into the factories."[35] Elsie McAlister remembered that in Globe-Miami, "World War II really brought about a great release for a lot of women because they took the places of the men in the mines here who went to war. And they didn't give up the jobs when the men came back."[36]

Jane Drees continued in her field of social work during the war, but she had a new "war-related" job. "In 1941, Phoenix was declared off-bounds [to employees of] Luke Air Force Base because of prostitution. The authorities [believed] it was necessary to take some action to clean up the situation. [Through] a private agency, I was given the responsibility of interviewing [any] woman who was picked up on a charge of any kind. The charge on which they were picked up was out of my hands completely, but I determine[d] what could be done with them, what dispensation should be taken after they were discharged."[37]

Elsie Dunn was a homemaker when she took a "Rosie the Riveter" job in aircraft manufacture, which she enjoyed even though conditions were not ideal:

✦   ✦   ✦

I was a saw operator for eighteen months at Goodyear Aircraft [during the war]. I just went down and applied for it, and I didn't get [to] saw at first because I had to earn that [and] train a little bit. I had a natural instinct with machinery.

[The] big majority [of workers] were women. And the men were paid more money than the women [for the same work]. They would bring in jobs and each one of us had a job to do. The man [who] sat [next to me] would take two days, and I would get mine done in eight hours. He got more money than I did per hour, and I said to the boss, I said, "How come George got to take two days to do this [and] I get it done in one? Why do you bring his [unfinished work back] to me?" He says, "I know you'll get it done."

[Unequal pay was] accepted at that time.[38]

✦   ✦   ✦

If the war opened opportunities for most women in Arizona, it completely changed the lives of Japanese-American women in the state. After Pearl Harbor, many believed all people of Japanese descent were essentially "enemy aliens." When President Franklin D. Roosevelt signed Executive Order 9066 early in 1942, all Japanese-Americans in the western half of the three Pacific Coast states and the southern third of Arizona were to be interned, to keep them away from the coastline and the large ship-building and aircraft factories.

The boundary designating the restricted zone in Arizona ran along Highway 95 from Ehrenberg, on the Arizona-California border, to Quartzite and east through Brenda and Salome. Then it continued along Highway 60 through Wickenburg, Surprise, Sun City, and Peoria. It ran through Phoenix along Grand Avenue and Van Buren Street, and then stretched through Tempe along Mill Avenue and Apache Boulevard, running through the center of Mesa. From Mesa it continued to Florence Junction, and Globe, where it extended along Highway 70 to Safford, and then Duncan on the Arizona-New Mexico border.[39]

Since the boundary ran right through communities, people living on one side of a street could remain, while friends across the street were interned. Half of the Japanese-American community in Arizona was sent to the Poston Camp in the dusty and shadeless desert and half remained in their homes. Some moved to avoid internment, even when it meant giving up their businesses. Mariyo Hikida and her husband made the painful decision to sell their farm and move rather than be interned. "At that time I was married and my husband was farming quite extensively, but it was all on the south side of the highway, so he had to just practically give everything away and move over. Many of the families took a great loss."[40]

Those Japanese-Americans who were interned faced tremendous hardships. The camps were makeshift affairs, in isolated areas, lacking any amenities and devoid of privacy. All able-bodied people were expected to work, and the pay scale was $19 or $16 a month, depending on the skill the job required. All jobs were under the supervision of Anglo administrators, but there were a large number of highly skilled jobs and professionals to fill them in each camp. The internees were to run everything, except the policy, in a model city arrangement. Ayako Kanemura's family held a wide range of jobs in Poston:

✦   ✦   ✦

First I wanted to find art work, but I didn't last too long because it wasn't very interesting so I worked in the mess hall, but that wasn't for me, so I went to the accounting department—time-keeping—and I enjoyed that, so I stayed there. We made out the payroll for Camps 1, 2 and 3, and then we'd send it out. I got $19.00. And then I got my dad's [monthly] clothing allowance which was $3.50 because I washed and ironed his clothes. So I had some extra money to spend. My dad learned to make *tofu* [pressed bean curd]. I recall he went to a shoe shop and then he was a block gardener, and then he enjoyed that. He got $16.00. [My sister] was secretary for the block manager; then she went to the optometry department. She was assistant optometrist; she fixed all the glasses and fitted them. That was $16.00.[41]

✦   ✦   ✦

Just as the war propelled women into the labor force and wrought havoc with many Japanese-American women's lives, internal familial tragedies also forced women into work, for better or worse. Married women who were full-time homemakers sometimes found themselves financially up against it when their husbands became sick or disabled. Additionally, several women were divorced and more were widowed. In all these cases, the women had to become the breadwinners for themselves and their families, as well as continuing to be the main homemakers. Exie Zieser worked before she was married but lost her job because she married. After several years, her husband went blind and lost his job when their three children were little. She immediately went back to work but felt she had no chance for job mobility because everyone depended on her and she could not take risks.[42] Similarly, Anne Bush faced her first job when her husband became ill: "My husband had a breakdown about 1944 and I had to go to work. I did have this degree, but I didn't have any work experience. [A friend] said, 'Go down to the welfare [office]. They don't pay very well, but they certainly do want people to work there.' I worked as a social worker under the State Merit System for ten or twelve years and then I was made a district supervisor and worked until I was 70. It was really quite a job to train and keep track of those people, and the case loads we had were stupendous."[43]

With far fewer resources because of her deeply regretted lack of education, Elsie Dunn also had to return to work after her husband's heart attack: "I needed to work because my husband had a coronary thrombosis. I got to work at the hospital [for] eight years. I didn't do practical nursing. I did the management of the laundry. I supervised twenty-one women and eight men. When I first went to work at the hospital, I [w]as a maid which paid $135 a month, six days a week. I finally got up to where I got $1 an hour, so some weeks I would work six days and some weeks I would work seven. My husband was in and out of the hospital and I had a child to keep, too, in school. That wasn't very much to get by with."[44]

As with husbands' illnesses, widowhood propelled women back into the paid labor force. Violet Irving became the sole owner of her husband's store upon his death and brought it out of a terrible downward slide caused by his long illness:

✦   ✦   ✦

I was the biggest coward that ever lived. I could have probably made some money after [paying off all] that [debt], but all I could think of was all those debts I'd sweated and paid, and I couldn't expand after that. I stayed in the Skull Valley store until 1962. For health reasons the doctor said I must sell, which broke my heart. I remained the Postmaster until 1971, when I was mandatorily retired.

A good part of my working life, [I] was on my own [because I was widowed three times]. It's just part of life. Even when I was married, I worked. I did my share as I could, and I never thought about it. I worked always. It was a job that had to be done and I did it. That was all.[45]

◆   ◆   ◆

At the age of 33, Lupe Hernandez was also widowed. She had to work to support herself and the nine children she raised, three of her own, four of her late husband's brothers and sisters, and two nieces. She always tried to work close to home, so she could keep track of the children; she never had money for child care:

◆   ◆   ◆

In those days there was no [state welfare] help, none. I went to look for work and the Americans would say to me, "We have work to be done, that you could do, but we don't have money to pay with." I would say, "But I know that I could do it for you, yes. I need something to buy food for my children with. I have children to support, and I can't work for nothing. I need something to take them to eat." I would leave in the morning, sometimes with nothing in my stomach, not even coffee, because we didn't have any. I went to look for work, and I came back like I left because there wasn't any more. When there was nothing, I even had to go up there past Esperanza. We would finish cleaning the house at twelve and sometimes they would give us a small plate, a little cup, a piece of bread and a weenie. That's the food that they gave us because, the poor things, I think that they too had little. We would eat it and go to another house. We would leave sometimes at five or six in the afternoon.

About five or seven of us women would go up there all together. We were almost all of us widows. We got together to work to support our children. Not one would say, "You go first." No indeed, we all went together and came back down together.

I worked washing and ironing. This porch had a bar from one wall to the other, and that's where I ironed and hung the clothes. That was my life, washing and ironing. We didn't have steam irons or anything like that. [We] heat[ed] the iron on the wood stove. I had everything the hard way, washboard and washtub. At night I washed in order to make it through the day. At midnight I would be hanging clothes. There were days that I didn't sleep more than a few hours. I would have liked to go to bed and sleep 'til nine. What hopes! By five o'clock I was already up. I worked very hard. There are some women here in Miami who tell me: "I worked so much." But they don't compare. I even went for firewood on the hill and carried it on my back. There was a man who would drive through here because he lived over there on the edge of town. Sometimes he would find me and put the firewood in his car and bring it for me. On my back, I had to bring firewood in order to cook the food, because I didn't have enough money [for fuel].

I worked a long time, cleaning rooms right nearby here, too. I managed because I was making just enough. In the morning I went in to clean rooms. From cleaning rooms I went to the store, [and] I left the store at four and I went to the restaurant and left it at midnight. [Sometimes I worked after midnight.] I worked at this restaurant washing dishes and cleaning tables.

I [also] packed tortillas [at] Martha Gomez' tortilla factory and I made menudo. I cleaned floors. They made the tortillas by machine, but we packed them in plastic bags. I worked there a long time, about three, maybe, about five years, until I got tired and I got a job with the state.

[But mostly I] cleaned houses, one a day. They were big houses. When they started to get to know me, they wouldn't leave me alone. They called me everywhere. When they started trusting me, they didn't let me go. "Come this day and come that day." They found out about me in thousands of ways. They could see that I didn't take anything. I left everything like it was. I cleaned and put things right away.[46]

✦   ✦   ✦

Widowed at sixty, Nora McKinney did not qualify for Social Security and suddenly found herself needing to work. She had been a ranch wife for twenty-one years, sometimes raising flowers for sale and working on the census, but she had not worked full-time for pay since she had married. She had taken up leather work as a hobby two years before her husband died, and as a widow she started selling her leather work and sewing for her livelihood. She sold the ranch and moved to Globe in 1954 where she took a course in hotel and motel management and found a job in a local motel, all the while selling her leather work all over the country and giving lessons to students in leather craft. When she lost her motel job, State Senator Polly Rosenthal got her a position with the state legislature running the mimeograph department. She worked there for six years until her retirement.[47]

Women approached retirement differently. The majority were pleased to retire and ready to move into a more leisurely life. Some were very unhappy, however, and agreed with Elsie Dunn: "When I went to sign up for my Social Security, it hurt me. [I felt I was] finished.[48] Similarly, Violet Irving resisted retirement:

✦   ✦   ✦

[In] 1971, I got the little slip that says "You have reached the mandatory" which I resented with every bone in my body. I wasn't ready to leave [being postmistress]. I hated it! I resented it terribly because I was in very good health and I would have liked to have worked a little longer. Had I been able to work another year, my retirement would have [been] enhanced.

My life was really worthwhile and beautiful [because of the] people that I associated with [at work]—friends, and business associates. That's what I miss most of all. I think that's the reason I'm dying on the vine of boredom today.[49]

✦   ✦   ✦

For many women, like Irene King, Winona Montgomery, Madge Copeland, and Irene Bishop, retirement was a time to pursue special interests, to continue and develop their volunteer work, and to travel. Most seemed happy with their lives. Edna Phelps discussed her retirement:

✦   ✦   ✦

Neither did I have much choice, nor was it a traumatic experience. I think it was because I had tapered off. Many people find it traumatic to leave their jobs because [they are] unaware of the fact that their jobs had been their social life. That was not my problem because I eased out of the picture. Another thing that I have done since retiring was doing newsletters for different organizations and researching local history, talking to old-timers. This has helped me with my social life. I've been in contact with people that way. And it has brought me friends because once in a while there's a little article in the paper about me, [which] brings telephone calls. Then I have people coming to look at my pictures and reading the notes that I have and talking to me about history. I enjoy it very much. I enjoy my retirement really.[50]

✦   ✦   ✦

Tillie Garten, who took up painting after her retirement, described her life with her husband: "[We] retired at the same time. He's here all day, busy with hobbies and we travel and have a good time. I have no regrets about my life, that's the point. I think that's what I can say."[51]

Women were vital workers in the growing territory and state of Arizona. They did a wide variety of jobs on their own and with their families. They worked in their homes, and they did important work in the community. Paid work was integral to their lives and central to the development of the state's economy. Since their work lives have ended, they have continued their community work and, for the most part, enjoy their leisure time as active "senior citizens."

REFLECTING ON CHANGE

✦

I simply think I have lived in a miracle age.
Benita Fennemore

Everyone who has lived from 1890 to 1980 has witnessed change, particularly the evolution of technology from, as one woman in our study said, horses and buggies to cars, to planes, to space shuttles. But Arizona pioneers also have seen settlement growth the likes of which very few people have ever encountered in a lifetime. Overwhelmingly, when we asked the women we interviewed to reflect on their lives, they focused on change, in Arizona, technology, historical events, and women's roles. During Clara Kimball's life, for instance, Phoenix went from a village of 3,152 in 1890 to a metropolitan area of 1,509,000 in 1980, and Arizona expanded from a raw territory of 88,243 to a sunbelt urban state of 2,718,425, one of the fastest growing in the nation. Technological development made that possible, too, especially the evolution of evaporative cooling and refrigeration.[1]

All of these women saw settlers conquer the desert, with individual homesteads at first, and then more recently with huge developments replete with lakes, lawns, and lavish landscaping. Many have real qualms about what will happen to Arizona with its continuing unbridled growth, which is often so at odds with the natural environment. Several spoke of the fragility of the desert, and many fondly remembered picnics in the wildflowers and natural beauty of the Salt River Valley, impossible to replicate, since one-and-a-half million people now live there. Several women were particularly concerned about the waste of water that new settlement has encouraged.

In addition to the migration and development that has defined Arizona since 1890, other national historical events have affected everyone in the state as well, and the women we interviewed were not immune to these events. For a few, one of their earliest public memories was the Armistice Day of World War I. But the two main historical events that had a real impact on their daily lives were the Depression, when all of the women had to cope with tough times, and World War II, when their home-front lives were all drastically altered. For many, the civil rights movement changed their lives as well, and Anglo, Black, and Indian women all commented on the lessening of discrimination against minorities and the ending of official segregation as a positive change.

The development of civil rights for minorities in Arizona helped spur women's rights, too. Reflecting national changes in women's lives, opportunities opened for women in Arizona and women's roles expanded.

Every woman discussed the changing status of women during their lifetimes, and nearly all were conflicted about contemporary women's lives. Several felt today's women, often including their granddaughters, had lost some quintessentially feminine qualities, but all believed women work hard and should be rewarded more for their efforts. When they were interviewed in 1981, most were opposed to the then-proposed Equal Rights Amendment, but all favored equal pay for equal work and more opportunities for women in the work place. Some dubbed themselves "feminists," but most did not, seeing the feminist label as inherently anti-male. Several bemoaned the necessity of their granddaughters' having to work while their children were little, and many saw a decline in the structure of the family because of the greater likelihood that women would work for pay while their children were young.

On the controversial question of abortion, the women over-whelmingly supported the notion of a woman's right to privacy to make that most difficult decision. None admitted to ever having had an abortion, and many were troubled by the idea of abortion, particularly as a form of birth control. Of the women who were asked, however, only one, a devout Catholic, absolutely opposed abortion. All of the others believed only the woman directly involved should make the decision with the advice of her doctor. Even politically conservative women did not believe the state had a right to intervene in such a private and personal decision.

When asked to reflect personally about their lives, most of the women were at ease and happy. None wanted to go back to the "good old days," before indoor plumbing, air conditioning, cars, and washing machines, but several would go back twenty or thirty years, when Phoenix, especially, was smaller and less urban—more comfortable. Survivors all, they had mastered change as well as seen it, and they looked forward to the twenty-first century.

When asked to reflect on their communities, all set a scene of a small, pioneer place before they launched into a tale of growth and development. Fern Johnson vividly described the Phoenix of her girlhood: "We went in a horse and buggy [in Phoenix]. It was hot. The pavement was real soft. Indians [sat in] the streets selling their products and men [with] tuberculosis [stood] around coughing and spitting. . . . At first there was no electricity [and so we had no cooling]. . . . People complained [and asked], 'how did you live?' and I say, 'what else were we to do?' We didn't know anything else to do, we just lived."[2]

Irene Bishop recalled of her childhood: "For years [Tempe was] just a little one-horse town. When we were children, my mother made about two trips to Phoenix a year [with a] horse and buggy [to] buy our new clothes and material. People always said Tempe was just a little school town and wouldn't amount to anything, but look at it today."[3]

Elsie Dunn recollected: "When we first came here [to Phoe-

nix], this was an agricultural and cattle town. That was what it
was built for. In springtime the desert was solid [with] beautiful
flowers. It was gorgeous. We used to go and pick flowers with a
horse and buggy."[4]

Jane Drees affirmed: "Growth [was] gradual up until the time
of World War II and then it was rather dramatic, sudden. In the
early days there were a great many health seekers came to Arizona, and they lived on the desert off the old Arizona canal.
When we hit 50,000, we really thought we had attained something in Phoenix. We were always very conscious of the growth
and had a lot of pride in the community."[5]

In rural Walker, Arizona, Violet Irving remembered how
neighbors shared in a time before both convenient supermarkets
and refrigerators. "We lived high enough in the mountains that
if you butchered a beef, you divided with your neighbor. When
the neighbor butchered, he divided with you, and that way you
had not too much. It was cool enough at night that you hung it
out and took it down in the daytime and laid it on the floor in the
cellar where it was cool and covered it over, and it'd stay cold
until you hung it out the next night, and that way you could keep
meat for quite a spell. We ate a lot of chicken in the summertime."[6]

Reflecting on the changes she had seen, Loretto Coles also discussed urban neighborliness in early Phoenix:

✦   ✦   ✦

We had wide open spaces and we could sit out in our yards and
not worry. We could enjoy [the] real Arizona, the openness.
People knew each other very well. They were competitive in
business, but it was small business. Now everything is so
tremendously big. On the other hand, we did not have advan-
tages. We had to go to Los Angeles for a lot of things, [includ-
ing] good medical care. Now we are known as a medical center. We also have plays, music, the symphony—all those things
we couldn't afford in the twenties or thirties. And they're
wonderful assets to Phoenix. We have better libraries. Our

historical sites have been improved so that they're wonderful to see. That part I love.[7]

✦   ✦   ✦

Fern Johnson recalled the changes she has seen on her Peoria farm and talked of her uneasiness about the future:

✦   ✦   ✦

Since electricity came in we have all of our appliances now [and] that makes things so much easier. We have become dependent on it. We farmers grieve over the loss of farming acreage and we say, "Where will the food come from?" We're very aware of the water system. We know our pump is going down every year. And the time will come that we will run out of water. We have so many people who do not know the value of water that is wasted. These new subdivisions insist that they have to have lakes. That lowers all the wells around them and what the future will be we do not know because the water is going down every year. But still people come and still all the cities around here grow.[8]

✦   ✦   ✦

Summing up the views of most of the women, Irene Bishop declared: "I've seen many changes during the years from horse and buggy to automobiles and planes, from palm leaf fans to re-frigeration, from kerosene lamps to electric lights, from wood stoves to gas or electric, from water kegs and wells to city water and modern plumbing, from dusty and muddy roads to pave-ment. I've seen good changes and I've seen bad changes. They talk about the good old days [but] I do not want to go back. I'd like to go back about twenty years, but not beyond that. Life was too hard."[9]

One of the major improvements several women addressed was an increase in interracial tolerance and a decrease in discrimina-tion and segregation. Jane Drees commented on the "much better relationship now between the Mexican-Americans and the An-glos [in Globe-Miami]" and particularly lauded school desegregation,[10] and Cecelia Sneezy was proud to be a part of Globe High School's innovative program to teach Apache youth their heritage, history, and language in a previously all-white school. Nevertheless, Sneezy, aware of the progress in integration and involved in helping Apache children stay in school, complained of the double-edged sword of integration: "Nowadays all of the small kids talk English. They don't talk their own language [Apache] anymore. I don't like this. It is not right. All of my children talk their own language and then English, but my grandkids are not like that. Some of them understand [Apache], but not all of them. They don't want to learn to talk in their own language. [They're] kind of ashamed."[11]

Providing a realistic assessment of both progress and resistance, Madge Copeland described her view of changing race relations in Arizona:

✦   ✦   ✦

[Discrimination still exists.] It has abated, you know, it's quieted, but it's still there. We'll never get out of all of it. [I'm] just thankful that progress has happened like it has. There are always some white people to help. They opened the way for us, but large numbers don't believe in that at all. They sure don't. We can go to any hotel, any restaurant—that used to be unthinkable, completely unthinkable, but now [they're] open for us to go. [Positions] have opened in government, in housing, and in labor for both Negro men and women. I think [discrimination] will always be here until the Lord turns everything to heaven as He said He would. I think it will always be here, but we don't have anything like as much as we used to have. Not anything like it.[12]

✦   ✦   ✦

Arizonans' work to end segregation and improve race relations was part of an important historical movement in this country. When asked what other historical events had an impact on their lives, several women spoke of World War I. Edna Phelps recalled: "During World War I, everyone felt involved because we all had at least a neighbor or a friend [or] a relative overseas. We watched the papers all the time for casualties. They were printed by name every day. We were rationed and allowed only two pounds of sugar per person per month. . . . Flour was not rationed in quantity, but [when] you bought any pound of flour you had to buy an equal amount of a substitute, either potato flour, rice flour, or corn meal."[13]

Elsie McAlister recounted: "I was either in the third or fourth grade during World War I, and I remember our teacher decided that the whole class should learn to knit, but I don't think [we] knitted anything except mufflers. . . . I remember when [the war] was over, they let school out and my father [took] us all to Globe in the car. We went down in front of the newspaper office, The *Arizona Record,* and as the news came in, the fire whistles and the horns [blew]. It was a big celebration."[14]

As young women, all were affected by the Depression. While most came through all right, they remembered it vividly their entire lives:

◆   ◆   ◆

The Depression years were pretty tough for us. I had started teaching in 1929 at a salary of $1250 a year; most of that was going into the family because I was still living at home. Living at home, I didn't have to pay rent, and they needed my help and my income. I would buy groceries and pay the taxes and buy gasoline.

Most of my money [went] to clothe myself decently for teaching, to buy insurance and gasoline for my car, and to help feed the family.

One experience made me so aware of the effect that the Depression was having on the general economy. We were in sight of the railroad that traveled between Tucson and Phoenix, and I made it a point over one weekend to count the men that were riding the rails on these cars every time a train went by. There would be ten or twelve trains a day including freight trains. I would count twenty-five to fifty men on top of freight cars or on flat cars riding toward Phoenix. Then the train that came back toward Tucson, there would be twenty-five to fifty on each car [and] I don't know how many inside the box cars. Back and forth these men were going in search of jobs from one part of the country to another.[15]

+   +   +

Benita Fennemore believed the Depression was easier in Phoenix, because, "[it] was small and I don't think we were affected with the bread lines and all that we [saw] and read [about] in New York and Chicago at that time." She continued: "We had some outstanding artists here under the W.P.A. work program. They were people who later became well known. We had the CCC, Civilian Conservation [Corps], to help with paths where people could hike around lakes and scenic places. Young people, who were otherwise unemployed, got small wages, and I thought some of those programs were excellent."[16]

The bombing of Pearl Harbor was the single most important historical memory for the women of this generation. Elizabeth Hovde remembered her shock: "It was a Sunday afternoon and we were having a birthday party for our little daughter. We were out in the yard under the trees and heard [about Pearl Harbor] on the radio. Of course, [I] was in shock and [thought] 'Why couldn't they have at least waited until after Christmas?' That was the first thing I said."[17]

Elsie McAlister recalled:

+   +   +

That Sunday afternoon when Pearl Harbor was bombed, we had been up to the Pinal mountains on a little ride. We had taken one of the neighborhood ladies with us, and when we came back her son came right away to tell us what had happened. We turned on our radio immediately and it stayed on for days. We felt it would be over in no time, just a matter of a few weeks.

Rationing was rather hard, particularly with growing children who wear out shoes so quickly. We had stamps for [shoes], for sugar, and gasoline. We had to discontinue going to the company doctor in Miami because we did not have enough gas to make runs like that.

We were issued a liberty cookbook [and] I tried my best to substitute. We used honey a great deal instead of sugar. And I did make some muffins with honey that my family liked, but most things we had to substitute they didn't care for. We missed the meat terribly. My family were always great meat eaters. It was very easy to plan a meal around a nice piece of meat and [it] was hard to fill in other things.[18]

✦   ✦   ✦

Pearl Harbor unleashed a flood of anti-Japanese feelings. Japanese goods were boycotted, and Japanese Americans faced strong prejudice, even when they were not interned. Loretto Coles, running the china department of her father's store, remembered: "I'd say [people had a] hatred of the 'Japs.' It happened I had a tremendous amount of Japanese china which was very competitive and very good really. There was no question [I] had to get rid of it immediately for $5, 10, or whatever because if people saw Japanese merchandise, they'd think you were pro-Japanese."[19]

Susie Sato painfully recalled what it was like to be a Japanese American in Mesa, Arizona, living in the "Free Zone." "The war came along and all of us destroyed anything that was Japanese, which was unfortunate. All things Japanese were discouraged. . . . In downtown Mesa there were a few other Japanese. If we met them, we were ashamed to bow to them because of what the Caucasian people would think. And we'd be ashamed to speak Japanese. I don't think we had anything to worry about, speaking Japanese, because we've lived there all our lives and we knew all the people, but just because of the atmosphere of the war."[20]

Several women had sons who were soldiers and daughters who were married to soldiers. Irene Bishop's son-in-law was in the Army Air Corps, initially training at William's Field, and Mary Moeur's son was in the army in New York City. Madge Copeland's son was drafted out of college into the army and her son-in-law was in the army, as well, leaving his wife home with her mother. Although it was a time of profound worry and fear, Madge was able to laugh at the fact that "she bore two children during that time. He would come back home on vacation. Whenever he did we could look for an increase in the family."[21]

Following the war, from the late forties to the present, the world changed enormously: America became a major world power; Arizona more than quadrupled its population; men walked on the moon; segregation ended; and women's lives were transformed. All of the women commented on what they felt about this transformation, and many felt a certain amount of conflict. To a person, they believed women deserve equal pay for equal work, but some expressed keen regret that women should be forced to leave the home, especially when they have children. On the other hand, many reveled in what they felt were new and exciting times for women and believed their granddaughters' lives would be better than their own. On both sides of the spectrum, however, there was real conflict about women's evolving roles, and the statements they made, and deeply felt, were often confusing and contradictory. Appreciative of the expanded opportunities available to women, Elizabeth Hovde said, "Women aren't expected to just stay home and wash and iron and cook and that sort of thing. They have so much more freedom. Even the clothes are less confining, easier to wear and more comfortable. . . . Women are free to have a larger choice of work. I'm firmly convinced that women should be paid the same wage as a man for doing the same work, whether it's an executive office or running a jack-hammer. If they do work the same, they should be paid the same. That's not always so. The freedom [women now have], I think it's great."[22]

On the other side, Anne Bush, who was a social worker for twenty-three years and enjoyed the status she received in her job, still believed it should be a man's world:

✦   ✦   ✦

I was brought up to think that men were leaders and I'm not aggressive or a feminist in any sense of the word. The best thing people can do is to have the man be the leader and that's my feelings still. People I associate with are very much opposed to the ERA [Equal Rights Amendment]. I don't know anybody

closely who is for it. I'm not in favor of ERA. I think the way
we have it set up now is perfectly all right. My daughter
went in the service, but she went because she wanted to. The
idea of drafting women, I don't get.

I guess that it is true that [women] are discriminated against,
but if men are doing their duty and providing for the family, so
their wife can stay home and take care of the children, they
should have more pay. I think it's too bad that so many women
have to go to work. I'm sorry that I had to go to work. My
brothers were just horrified when I went to work. It's too bad
that the economy makes it so women have to work. That's
what I feel about it. My girls both work, but I think it would
be pretty nice if they didn't have to.[23]

✦   ✦   ✦

Exemplary of the women who felt a lot of conflict over wom-
en's changing roles, their own life experiences, and the opportunities now open to women, Exie Zieser declared:

✦   ✦   ✦

I don't think much of [the woman's movement. However,] I
think women should be paid the same money as men for
the same work, but as far as women getting out and digging
ditches and being in the army, women were never equipped for
that, I don't think. Of course, I get out and dig ditches and
things, but I don't think it was ever intended for women to do
the same work as men.

I believe in equal pay for equal work, which I never did get.
After I'd been [in my job at Swift's] for five or six years, they
brought a guy in and paid him more than they paid me [for]
doing the same work and he couldn't [do it as well as I].[24]

✦   ✦   ✦

More positively, but still acknowledging the difficulties
women face, Benita Fennemore said:

✦   ✦   ✦

Each woman has to find her own way, her own change. And
I'm afraid women decide that they must change their way
of life because it is now expected of them [to be] liberated.
Maybe for one woman it is right, for another, it is not. A
woman who attempts a good marriage and children and career
undoubtedly has problems. She may be capable of solving
them [but maybe not].

I think women's role in society is changing. Women are now
occupying positions in every walk of life, not just jobs as
earners but in the highest echelons. We are probably going to
have a woman, Sandra Day O'Conner, on the United States
Supreme Court, and I think that's great, that's wonderful. I
think women have a great deal more to offer to society than
they were allowed to offer before. I think there will be a woman
president one day.[25]

✦   ✦   ✦

Thoughtfully reflecting on the evolving roles of women and
men in her lifetime, why some things have changed and some
have not, Violet Irving commented: "I think that we hear of very
few women who have major roles, but what in the world would
those men who are making history have done without the
women that kept them going and bolstered them and kept the
home fires burning? . . . I think that women filled the place that
they could fill. They couldn't mine; they couldn't go out and do
the things that the men did. They couldn't fight, but they did
what they could do. My feeling is that women could do anything
within their brains or energy."[26]

On the specific women's issues of access to birth control and
abortion, the women were overwhelmingly in favor of a woman's right to control her reproductive life. Tillie Garten, one of
the strongest proponents of abortion, said clearly, "I am for abortion. I think everybody has a right to decide for themselves. I
don't think it should be a federal law or a state law or a city law.
I think it should be an individual law."[27] But Jane Drees, a Republican Party activist, voiced the most common position when
she said, "I'm not a pro-abortionist. Neither am I an anti-
abortionist. I think there are many times when abortion probably

would be the answer. But I think it's a matter of personal opinion. It's an individual problem. I don't think it should be made a national problem. Abortion is strictly an individual matter between the husband and wife and their physician."[28]

Asked to reflect on their personal lives, rather than the large questions of women's roles and politics, most seemed basically happy. Some had real emotional wounds, the worst from the death of children and spouses, but most seemed peaceful and at ease. Some might have made different choices; some wished they had had more opportunities; but, all in all, few expressed real regrets about their lives.

Elsie McAlister believes: "The last years of our lives together have been the happiest time of my life. We are very happy together. We do things together. And I was happy as a child. I didn't realize all the hardships that we all went through. You look back on your memories; the birth of your children, each one was an adventure."[29]

For most of the women, raising their children was their clearest happiness. Over and over again, women referred to the birth of their children as the happiest days of their lives and nearly all presented child rearing as a real joy. Typically, Mary Moeur believed, "The very, very happiest time of my life [was] the day I got married and the day my boy was born. That was such a wonderful day—to see that little baby! It's quite something really."[30] And Elsie Dunn, who had a hard life, maintained, "The most happiness that I think I've ever known [was] tak[ing] care of my children and bring[ing] them up. Outside of that, [I've] had very few [happy times]."[31]

Taking a somewhat different stance, Edna Phelps believes she has found her happiness in the ways she has dealt with change and has grown in her life:

✦   ✦   ✦

I've been a late bloomer. My political attitudes have changed radically. My thinking has deepened about social questions, and I'm very much involved in reading and thinking about the

women's movement. I have very deep feelings [in favor of] the
ERA.

I am thinking much more than I did in my earlier life about
all social problems, poverty, minorities and their position in
our society, unions, and the role of education in the lives
of both men and women but particularly women. If I had to
trade off anything in my life, the last [thing] I would trade
[would be] my college education. [It] has been very valuable to
me, not necessarily financially, but in [my] ability to meet
problems and think objectively, [to] strive to see both
viewpoints.[32]

◆　　◆　　◆

Through their words and their families' stories, the women we
have interviewed have given us a vision of their lives and changing Arizona. They told us funny stories and sad ones; they explained their work and what it meant to them to be a neighbor.
They are all survivors and their stories show a sturdy persever-
ance, which may not reflect the lives of those who came and then
moved on.

The first issue all had to face was how they related to the desert:
why did they arrive in Arizona and what did the landscape mean
to them? Slightly less than half of the women were born here and
have always lived here. For them, Arizona has always been
home. The remaining sixteen migrated in, most as young girls
and some as young women. Twelve came to Arizona as members
of families, but four of the women came themselves as young
adults, mistresses of their fates, ready for a desert adventure. For
all of the immigrants, Arizona was a strange new land, dry and
hot and stark, which some loved on sight and others feared and
disliked. The women's responses to the desert varied by their personalities, as well as their circumstances for coming, but they all
ultimately came to love it and consider it home. Common to
both the natives and the immigrants was the theme of betterment: all saw in Arizona a chance for economic advancement,
better health, or religious mission.

Growing up in Arizona was a real pioneer experience, rough

and primitive. Town women's lives were somewhat easier than rural women's, but all their lives were made of hard work. The women we interviewed grew up with chores that were real and which aided the family economy if they lived on a farm or ranch. All learned women's traditional work from their mothers, aunts, and grandmothers. Part of women's work was caring for their families' health, and many learned home remedies and healing, as well as cooking, cleaning, and laundering.

Schooling was important across class and ethnic group, and families often made real sacrifices to keep their children in school. Our women were relatively highly educated for the time, with all but two finishing high school. Minority women had a profoundly different school experience from Anglo women, with Indian girls having to leave home to attend boarding schools, Hispanics experiencing de facto segregation, and Blacks being segregated by law.

Upon leaving school, most of the women's adult lives were centered in home and family. While three women remained single, the rest married and most had children. Raising their children and running their households defined their lives. While marriage was a nearly universal experience, it was often broken by divorce or death. Many women spent at least some of their adult lives supporting themselves and other family members. Even the women who remained single often had family responsibilities for nieces and nephews or aging parents.

Regardless of marital status, as adults, all of the women were also involved in a phenomenal range of community activities. Most of the social and artistic institutions we enjoy today had their origins in women's volunteer work. Many of the women considered their community work to be their job and gave it the standing in their lives that their husbands gave to their paid work. For most, volunteer activities also provided tremendous pleasure and a social community of women. Without exception, moreover, they saw their volunteer work with their churches, schools, children, social agencies, political parties, and cultural institutions as important work that would make Arizona a better place to live.

In addition to their volunteer work, all of the women worked for pay, at least for part of their lives. Some worked as children, and all worked as adults, though most dropped out of the paid labor force if they married and had children. Changes in family status sometimes pushed married women back into the labor force and, of course, the single women remained paid workers all of their lives. Women's jobs tended to be traditionally stereotyped and few opportunities opened in new areas until World War II factory production brought women into nontraditional industrial work. Women's work constituted a substantial amount of the family income, and women worked for the same reasons men did, to support their families.

Focusing on the entire vista of their lives, the women we interviewed came back again and again to a sense of amazement that they had lived and grown through such a changing world. Even though their lives differed materially, Benita Fennemore summed up this common sense of wonder and happiness that most of the women expressed:

✦   ✦   ✦

I think I've had a wonderful life. People in this day and age worry about all these things and I say, "There is always something to worry about." I've lived through two [world] wars, and that's the tragic thing and I hope and pray that someday the nations can learn to love one another. But outside of the wars, I think I've lived a very interesting life, not a celebrity's life, I've had a very modest life in many ways. But, gee whiz! I've told you about driving around in a surrey and horse and buggy and then we got our first car. I can remember learning to drive when I was thirteen or fourteen [and] I've lived to see from no traffic to too much traffic. I think the space age has been the most exciting of all. I just recently returned from Washington, and the first time I went to the Smithsonian, they had an exhibit on Charles Lindbergh's "Spirit of St. Louis" and the Wright Brothers' plane, and now you go and here [are] all these space labs. And I stood there the other day looking in one of the space capsules, and I thought, it's just so exciting that sometimes I can hardly believe it. I can't comprehend it. I don't actually comprehend television [either]. Again, that's an innovation in my lifetime. Back when I was a child, there were silent movies and then we got the spoken word on the screen and then radio and television. Here I sit and watch some event that's taking place maybe in Germany or England, and it's all on satellite. There it is over there and here I am: I don't understand how it even functions. I simply think I have lived in a miracle age. Scientifically, I am not able to comprehend these things and yet I accept them with great joy because they are really miracles. I think that medicine is also in the miracle age. There are hip implants, and heart and lung transplants, [and] patients walk out of hospitals, travel and do all kinds of perfectly normal work. We are living in the miracle age: that's my answer to you. I've had a very interesting and full life—every bit of it's been very good.[33]

✦   ✦   ✦

While some of the women had a less sanguine view of their lives, most of them felt lucky to have lived through these changes, just as Benita Fennemore did. And all of them and their stories are a part of Arizona's history. In listening to their voices, we have begun to envision what life was like for all the people in Arizona and how the state we know today was formed.

NOTES

✦

PREFACE

1. Corky Bush, Katherine Jensen, and Mary Aickin Rothschild, "Three Generations of an Oral History-Readers Theater Project," *Frontiers: A Journal of Women's Studies* 7, no. 1 (1983), 80–90.

2. Corlann Gee Bush, "The Way We Weren't: Images of Women and Men in Cowboy Art," *The Women's West,* Susan Armitage and Elizabeth Jameson (Norman: University of Oklahoma Press, 1987), 19–33.

3. See, for instance, Marshall Trimble, *Arizona: A Calvalcade of History* (Tucson, Ariz.: Treasure Chest Publications, 1989), and Odie Faulk, *Arizona: A Short History* (University of Oklahoma Press, 1988).

INTRODUCTION: FRAMING ARIZONA WOMEN'S HISTORY

1. The Selected Bibliography on p. 161 cites some of the best books in western women's history and indicates the recent growth in the field.

2. Julie Roy Jeffrey, *Frontier Women: The Trans-Mississippi West, 1840–1890* (New York: Hill and Wang, 1979).

3. Barbara Welter, "The Cult of True Womanhood," *American Quarterly* 18 (Summer 1966), 131–75.

4. Sandra L. Myres, *Westering Women and the Frontier Experience, 1800–1915* (Albuquerque, New Mexico: University of New Mexico Press, 1982).

5. Ruth B. Moynihan, Susan Armitage, and Christiane Fischer Dichamp, *So Much to Be Done: Women Settlers on the Mining and Ranching Frontier* (Lincoln, Nebr.: University of Nebraska Press, 1990), xiii.

6. John Mack Faragher, *Women and Men on the Overland Trail* (New Haven, Conn., 1979), and Lillian Schlissel, *Women's Diaries of the Westward Journey* (New York: Schocken Books, 1982).

7. Henry P. Walker and Don Bufkin, *Historical Atlas of Arizona* (Norman, Okla.: University of Oklahoma: 1989), 42 and 45.

8. Nat de Gennera, ed., *Arizona Statistical Abstract, 1979 Edition* (Tucson, Ariz.: Division of Economic and Business Research, The University of Arizona), 21–22.

9. Walker and Bufkin, *Historical Atlas*, 60–61; U.S. Department of Commerce, Bureau of the Census, *Characteristics of the Population, 1970 Census of Population,* Arizona (Washington, D.C.: Government Printing Office, 1973), Table 1, 7.

10. Bradford Luckingham, *The Urban Southwest: A Profile History of Albuquerque, El Paso, Phoenix and Tucson* (El Paso: Texas Western Press; University of Texas, El Paso, 1982); Bradford Luckingham, "Urban Development in Arizona: The Rise of Phoenix," *Journal of Arizona History* 22 (Summer 1981), 197-234; Bradford Luckingham, *Phoenix: The History of a Southwestern Metropolis* (Tucson: University of Arizona Press, 1989).

11. Susan Johnson, "Women's Households and Relationships in the Mining West: Central Arizona, 1863–1873," Master's Thesis (Tempe, Ariz.: Arizona State University, 1984), 123–27.

12. Rosalie Crowe and Diane Tod, eds., *Arizona Women's Hall of Fame* (Phoenix, Ariz.: Arizona Historical Society, 1986), 51–53.

13. Meredith Snapp, "Defeat the Democrats: The Arizona Campaigns of the Congressional Union for Woman Suffrage," Master's Thesis (Tempe, Ariz.: Arizona State University, 1976), 27–46; Meredith A. Snapp, "Defeat the Democrats: Union for Woman Suffrage in Arizona, 1914–1916," *Journal of the West* 14 (October 1975), 131–39.

14. Snapp, "Defeat the Democrats: The Arizona Campaigns…," 27–46.

15. Ibid.

16. Carrie Chapman Catt and Nettie Rogers Shuler, *Woman Suffrage and Politics: The Inside Story of the Suffrage Movement* (Seattle: University of Washington Press, 1970), 176–77; and Snapp, "Defeat the Democrats: The Arizona Campaigns…," 37.

17. Catt and Shuler, *Woman Suffrage and Politics*, entire; Aileen Krad-

itor, *The Ideas of the Woman Suffrage Movement, 1890–1920* (New York: W. W. Norton and Co., 1981).

18. Mary Aickin Rothschild and Pamela Claire Hronek, "A History of Arizona Women's Politics," in Rita Mae Kelly, ed., *Women and the Arizona Political Process* (Lanham, Md.: University Press of America, 1988), 5–20.

19. Department of Commerce, Bureau of the Census, *Fourteenth Census of the United States: 1920, Population* (Washington, D.C.: Government Printing Office, 1922), 1048–1053, 1068; Department of Commerce, Bureau of the Census, *Fifteenth Census of the United States: 1930, Population* (Washington, D.C.: Government Printing Office, 1932), 356.

COMING TO THE DESERT

1. Anne Bush, interview conducted by Rose Diaz, Summer 1981, Phoenix, Arizona, (hereinafter, Anne Bush), 4.

2. Mae Wills, interview conducted by Linda Salmon, Summer 1981, Globe, Arizona, (hereinafter, Mae Wills), 1.

3. Brenda Meckler, interview conducted by Rose Diaz, Summer 1981, Phoenix, Arizona, (hereinafter, Brenda Meckler), 7.

4. Fern Johnson, interview conducted by Pamela Hronek, Fall 1981, Peoria, Arizona, (hereinafter, Fern Johnson), 1.

5. Edna Brazill, interview conducted by Pamela Hronek, Summer 1981, Phoenix, Arizona, (hereinafter, Edna Brazill), 2.

6. Elsie Dunn, interview conducted by Pamela Hronek, Summer 1981, Phoenix, Arizona, (hereinafter, Elsie Dunn), 6.

7. Violet Irving, interview conducted by Pamela Hronek, Summer 1981, Mesa, Arizona, (hereinafter, Violet Irving), 1.

8. Loretto Coles, interview conducted by Pamela Hronek, Summer 1981, Phoenix, Arizona, (hereinafter, Loretto Coles), 1–2.

9. Clara Kimball, interview conducted by Pamela Hronek, Summer 1981, Mesa, Arizona, (hereinafter, Clara Kimball), 1.

10. Edna Brazill, 1.

11. Benita Fennemore, interview conducted by Pamela Hronek, Fall 1981, Phoenix, Arizona, (hereinafter, Benita Fennemore), 3.

12. Madge Copeland, interview conducted by Maria Hernandez, Summer 1981, Phoenix, Arizona, (hereinafter, Madge Copeland), 11–12.

13. Fern Johnson, 1.

14. Charlie Daniels, interview conducted by Evelyn Cooper, Spring 1981, (hereinafter, Charlie Daniels), Tape 2, Side A.

15. Marjorie Mandel, interview conducted by Rose Diaz, Summer 1981, Tempe, Arizona, (hereinafter, Marjorie Mandel), 3.

16. Tillie Garten, interview conducted by Pamela Hronek, Summer 1981, Tempe, Arizona, (hereinafter, Tillie Garten), 1.

17. Loretto Coles, 1–2.

18. Brenda Meckler, 8.

19. Edna Phelps, interview conducted by Linda Salmon, Summer 1981, Phoenix, Arizona, (hereinafter, Edna Phelps), 11–14.

20. Sallie Lewis, interview conducted by Linda Salmon, Fall 1981, Scottsdale, Arizona, (hereinafter, Sallie Lewis), 3.

21. Fern Johnson, 1–2, 6.

22. Benita Fennemore, 12.

23. Brenda Meckler, 8.

24. Elsie McAlister, interview conducted by Rose Diaz, Summer 1981, Globe, Arizona, (hereinafter, Elsie McAlister), 1.

25. Veora Johnson, interview conducted by Maria Hernandez, Summer 1981, Mesa, Arizona, (hereinafter, Veora Johnson), 2.

26. Mary Moeur, interview conducted by Rose Diaz, Summer 1981, Tempe, Arizona, (hereinafter, Mary Moeur), 1.

27. Edna Phelps, 10–13.

28. Clara Kimball, 3.

29. Fern Johnson, 37.

30. Elizabeth Hovde, interview conducted by Linda Salmon, Summer 1981, Mesa, Arizona, (hereinafter, Elizabeth Hovde), 31.

31. Irma West, interview conducted by Linda Salmon, Summer 1981, Mesa, Arizona, (hereinafter, Irma West), 36–37.

GROWING UP IN ARIZONA

1. Benita Fennemore, 5–6.

2. Edna Phelps, 4.

3. Sallie Lewis, 4.

4. Anne Bush, 4.

5. Fern Johnson, 8–9.

6. Ibid., 8.

7. Clara Kimball, 5.

8. Violet Irving, 15, 17.

9. Ibid., 18.

10. Cecelia Sneezy, interview conducted by Mary Rothschild, Fall 1986, Globe, Arizona, (hereinafter, Cecelia Sneezy), 3, 19.

11. Edna Phelps, 10–11.

12. Benita Fennemore, 10.
13. Elsie McAlister, 3–4.
14. Loretto Coles, 7.
15. Ruby Estrada, interview conducted by Maria Hernandez, Summer 1981, Phoenix, Arizona, (hereinafter, Ruby Estrada), 3.
16. Ibid., 19.
17. Clara Kimball 12–13.
18. Elsie Dunn, 6.
19. Clara Kimball, 6.
20. Elsie Dunn, 4.
21. Clara Kimball, 2.
22. Benita Fennemore, 4.
23. Sallie Lewis, 8.
24. Ibid., 15.
25. Cecelia Sneezy, 7.
26. Clara Kimball, 15, 22.
27. Fern Johnson, 30.
28. Clara Kimball, 14.
29. Loretto Coles, 6.
30. Elsie McAlister, 27.
31. Ibid., 28.
32. Edna Brazill, 4.
33. Irma West, 23.
34. Ibid.
35. Ibid.
36. Irene Bishop, interview conducted by Rose Diaz, Summer 1981, Phoenix, Arizona, 8.
37. Fern Johnson, 10.
38. Clara Kimball, 23.
39. Edna Phelps, 29.
40. Clara Kimball, 8–10.
41. Irma West, 22.
42. Elsie McAlister, 1.
43. Elizabeth Hovde, 20, 9.
44. Benita Fennemore, 23.
45. Clara Kimball, 8, 10.
46. Violet Irving, 5.
47. Irma West, 12.
48. Anne Bush, 4.
49. Benita Fennemore, 7.

50. Sallie Lewis, 7–8, 11, 22–23.

51. Cecelia Sneezy, 3, 6–7.

52. Ruby Estrada, 6.

53. Irene King, interview conducted by Maria Hernandez, Summer 1981, Phoenix, Arizona, (hereinafter, Irene King), 3, 11–12.

54. Ibid., 30.

55. Valerie Matsumoto, "'Shikata Ga Nai': Japanese American Women in Central Arizona, 1910–1978," (unpublished honor's thesis, Arizona State University, May, 1978), interview with Susie Sato, February 10, 1978, Tempe, Arizona, 20–21.

56. Exie Zieser, interview conducted by Linda Salmon, Summer 1981, Phoenix, Arizona, (hereinafter, Exie Zieser), 30.

57. Ruby Estrada, 10.

58. Irene Bishop, 13–14.

59. Fern Johnson, 12–13.

60. Irene King, 8.

61. Cecelia Sneezy, 5.

62. Exie Zieser, 15–16.

63. Edna Phelps, 52.

64. Elsie McAlister, 11.

65. Lupe Hernandez, interview conducted by Maria Hernandez, Summer 1981, Miami, Arizona, (hereinafter, Lupe Hernandez), 6–7.

66. Irma West, 9.

67. Edna Phelps, 7.

68. Mae Wills, 12.

69. Benita Fennemore, 16–17.

70. Ruby Estrada, 12.

71. Ibid.

72. Fern Johnson, 15.

DOING WHAT THE DAY BROUGHT

1. Elsie Dunn, 7–8.

2. Irma West, 17.

3. Elsie McAlister, 10–11.

4. Edna Brazill, 5.

5. Irene Bishop, 17.

6. Ruby Estrada, 11.

7. Cecelia Sneezy, 3.

8. Mary Moeur, 2.

9. Benita Fennemore, 24.

10. Clara Kimball, 18.

11. Ibid., 24.

12. Irene Bishop, 19.

13. Brenda Meckler, 13.

14. Fern Johnson, 20.

15. Ruby Estrada, 20.

16. Elsie Dunn, 22.

17. Charlie Daniels, Tape 1, Side A.

18. Elizabeth Hovde, 23.

19. Elsie Dunn, 23.

20. Irma West, 40.

21. Mae Wills, 26.

22. Nora McKinney, interview conducted by Rose Diaz, Summer 1981, Globe, Arizona, (hereinafter, Nora McKinney), 8.

23. Fern Johnson, 23–26.

24. Elizabeth Hovde, 42.

25. Benita Fennemore, 23–24.

26. Judith Walzer Leavitt, *Brought to Bed: Childbearing in America, 1750–1950* (New York: Oxford University Press, 1986); Catherine M. Scholten, "On the Importance of the Obstetric Art, Changing Customs of Childbirth in America 1750–1825," *William and Mary Quarterly* 34 (July 1971, 426–46); Nancy Schrom Dye, "History of Childbirth in America," *Signs* 6, no. 1 (Autumn, 1980), 97–108; Mary Melcher "'Women's Matters': Prenatal Care, Birth Control and Childbirth in Rural Montana, 1910–1940," unpublished paper presented at Twentieth Century Western Women's History Research Conference, Arizona State University, October 20, 1989.

27. Clara Kimball, 19–20.

28. Sallie Lewis, 34–36.

29. Ibid., 33–34.

30. Cecelia Sneezy, 16–17.

31. Nora McKinney, 23.

32. Edna Brazill, 37.

33. Marjorie Mandel, 28.

34. Benita Fennemore, 25.

35. Elsie McAlister, 12.

36. Edna Phelps, 53.

37. Mae Wills, 31.

38. Fern Johnson, 29–30.

39. Mae Wills, 31.

40. Elsie Dunn, 27.
41. Exie Zieser, 36–37.
42. Lupe Hernandez, 16.
43. Fern Johnson, 36.
44. Clara Kimball, 29.
45. Edna Phelps, 26.
46. Tillie Garten, 12–13.
47. Loretto Coles, 10, 15–16.
48. Winona Montgomery, interview conducted by Linda Salmon, Summer 1981, Phoenix, Arizona, (hereinafter, Winona Montgomery), 57.
49. Violet Irving, 21.
50. Ibid., 23–24.
51. Mary Moeur, 29–30.
52. Lupe Hernandez, 32.

BUILDING ARIZONA'S COMMUNITIES

1. Mary Melcher, "The Phoenix Civil Rights Movement: Black and White Collaboration, 1950–1970," unpublished paper, 1990, entire.
2. Edna Brazill, 28.
3. Benita Fennemore, 29–32.
4. Edna Brazill, 28.
5. Irma West, 55.
6. Madge Copeland, 43.
7. Irene Bishop, 27.
8. Mary Moeur, 21.
9. Jane Drees, interview conducted by Pamela Hronek, Summer 1981, Globe, Arizona, (hereinafter, Jane Drees), 20.
10. Edna Phelps, 36.
11. Fern Johnson, 36.
12. Violet Irving, 25.
13. Ibid., 25–26.
14. Ibid., 26–27.
15. Ibid., 26–29.
16. Benita Fennemore, 29.
17. Marjorie Mandel, 22.
18. Loretto Coles, 28–29.
19. Edna Brazill, 16–18.
20. Irene King, 10, 42.
21. Benita Fennemore, 31.

22. Exie Zieser, 56.
23. Benita Fennemore, 32–33.
24. Loretto Coles, 29.
25. Benita Fennemore, 30.
26. Mary Moeur, 23; Irene Bishop, 28–29.
27. Fern Johnson, 35.
28. Irene Bishop, 26–27.
29. Brenda Meckler, 16.
30. Marjorie Mandel, 35.
31. Irma West, 55.
32. Sallie Lewis, 39–40.
33. Marjorie Mandel, 34.
34. Edna Brazill, 15.
35. Elise Dunn, 14.
36. Cecelia Sneezy, 8–9.
37. Irene King, 77; Anne Bush, 29; Winona Montgomery, 38–39.
38. Loretto Coles, 26.
39. Irma West, 30.
40. Irene King, 45.
41. Cecelia Sneezy, 12–13.
42. Madge Copeland, 15–16; Mary Melcher, "Madge Copeland and Placida Garcia Smith: Community Organizers, Phoenix, Arizona 1930–1960," unpublished paper, 3–10.
43. Jane Drees, 15.
44. Edna Phelps, 60–61.
45. Madge Copeland, 33–34.
46. Ibid., 34.

WORKING FOR PAY IN A MAN'S WORLD

1. Clara Kimball, 13–14; Elsie Dunn, 6; Ruby Estrada, 19.
2. Edna Phelps, 17.
3. Elizabeth Hovde, 26; Irene King, 8.
4. Jane Drees, 5.
5. Elizabeth Hovde, 37.
6. Fern Johnson, 24.
7. Mary Moeur, 15–16.
8. Irene Bishop, 7, 16–21.
9. Irma West, 37.
10. Edna Brazill, 14.
11. Violet Irving, 14, 33.

12. Loretto Coles, 18, 21.

13. Ibid., 24.

14. Edna Phelps, 23.

15. Ibid., 25.

16. Jane Drees, 8–9.

17. Madge Copeland, 17–18, 21–24.

18. Elsie McAlister, 15; Benita Fennemore, 18.

19. Edna Brazill, 3, 5.

20. Elsie McAlister, 15.

21. Benita Fennemore, 24.

22. Edna Phelps, 56–58.

23. Ibid., 21.

24. Winona Montgomery, entire.

25. Veora Johnson, 1, 3–4.

26. Mary Melcher, "The Phoenix Civil Rights Movement...," 6–8.

27. Irene King, 22, 25.

28. Ibid., entire.

29. Charlie Daniels, 17.

30. Fern Johnson, 11.

31. Elsie McAlister, 34.

32. Cecelia Sneezy, 4–5, 19–20; Mary Rothschild, untaped interviews with Karen Huselid, Chandler, Arizona, 1986.

33. Clara Kimball, 25.

34. Benita Fennemore, 28.

35. Irene Bishop, 12.

36. Elsie McAlister, 33.

37. Jane Drees, 8.

38. Elsie Dunn, 17–18.

39. Valerie Matsumoto, interview with Susie Sato, "'Shikata Ga Nai'", 23–24.

40. Valerie Matsumoto, interview with Mariyo Hikida, October, 1976, Tempe, Arizona, "'Shikata Ga Nai,'" 24.

41. Valerie Matsumoto, interview with Ayako Kanemura, March 10, 1978, Tempe, Arizona, "'Shikata Ga Nai,'" 31–32.

42. Exie Zieser, 35–36.

43. Anne Bush, 20.

44. Elsie Dunn, 16.

45. Violet Irving, 10, 44.

46. Lupe Hernandez, 13, 16–17.

47. Nora McKinney, 18, 30–32.

48. Elsie Dunn, 33.
49. Violet Irving, 41–42.
50. Edna Phelps, 35.
51. Tillie Garten, 18.

REFLECTING ON CHANGE

1. Walker and Bufkin, 60–61.
2. Fern Johnson, 37.
3. Irene Bishop, 15.
4. Elsie Dunn, 34.
5. Jane Drees, 15.
6. Violet Irving, 32.
7. Loretto Coles, 35–36.
8. Fern Johnson, 39.
9. Irene Bishop, 39.
10. Jane Drees, 11–12.
11. Cecelia Sneezy, 13.
12. Madge Copeland, 32.
13. Edna Phelps, 14.
14. Elsie McAlister, 31.
15. Edna Phelps, 57–58.
16. Benita Fennemore, 31.
17. Elizabeth Hovde, 60.
18. Elsie McAlister, 32.
19. Loretto Coles, 40.
20. Valerie Matsumoto, interview with Susie Sato, "'Shikata Ga Nai'" 34.
21. Madge Copeland, 31.
22. Elizabeth Hovde, 65–66.
23. Anne Bush, 31–35.
24. Exie Zieser, 26.
25. Benita Fennemore, 26.
26. Violet Irving, 34.
27. Tillie Garten, 28.
28. Jane Drees, 20.
29. Elsie McAlister, 30.
30. Mary Moeur, 45.
31. Elsie Dunn, 38.
32. Edna Phelps, 32.
33. Benita Fennemore, 35–36.

BIBLIOGRAPHY

✦

ORAL HISTORY INTERVIEWS

Irene Bishop, interview conducted by Rosemary Diaz, Summer 1981, Phoenix, Arizona

Edna Brazill, interview conducted by Pamela Hronek, Fall 1981, Peoria, Arizona

Anne Bush, interview conducted by Rose Diaz, Summer 1981, Phoenix, Arizona

Loretto Coles, interview conducted by Pamela Hronek, Summer 1981, Phoenix, Arizona

Madge Copeland, interview conducted by Maria Hernandez, Summer 1981, Phoenix, Arizona

Charlie Daniels, interview conducted by Evelyn Cooper, Spring 1981, Phoenix, Arizona

Jane Drees, interview conducted by Pamela Hronek, Summer 1981, Globe, Arizona

Elsie Dunn, interview conducted by Pamela Hronek, Summer 1981, Phoenix, Arizona

Ruby Estrada, interview conducted by Maria Hernandez, Summer 1981, Phoenix, Arizona

Benita Fennemore, interview conducted by Pamela Hronek, Fall 1981, Phoenix, Arizona

Tillie Garten, interview conducted by Pamela Hronek, Summer 1981, Tempe, Arizona

Lupe Hernandez, interview conducted by Maria Hernandez, Summer 1981, Miami, Arizona

Elizabeth Hovde, interview conducted by Linda Salmon, Summer 1981, Mesa, Arizona

Karen Huselid, untaped interviews conducted by Mary Rothschild, Fall 1986, Chandler, Arizona

Violet Irving, interview conducted by Pamela Hronek, Summer 1981, Mesa, Arizona

Fern Johnson, interview conducted by Pamela Hronek, Fall 1981, Peoria, Arizona

Veora Johnson, interview conducted by Maria Hernandez, Summer 1981, Mesa, Arizona

Clara Kimball, interview conducted by Pamela Hronek, Summer 1981, Mesa, Arizona

Irene King, interview conducted by Maria Hernandez, Summer 1981, Phoenix, Arizona

Sallie Lewis, interview conducted by Linda Salmon, Fall 1981, Scottsdale, Arizona

Marjorie Mandel, interview conducted by Rose Diaz, Summer 1981, Tempe, Arizona

Brenda Meckler, interview conducted by Rose Diaz, Summer 1981, Phoenix, Arizona

Elsie McAlister, interview conducted by Rose Diaz, Summer 1981, Globe, Arizona

Nora McKinney, interview conducted by Rose Diaz, Summer 1981, Globe, Arizona

Mary Moeur, interview conducted by Rose Diaz, Summer 1981, Tempe, Arizona

Winona Montgomery, interview conducted by Linda Salmon, Summer 1981, Phoenix, Arizona

Edna Phelps, interview conducted by Linda Salmon, Summer 1981, Phoenix, Arizona

Cecelia Sneezy, interview conducted by Mary Rothschild, Fall 1986, Globe, Arizona

Irma West, interview conducted by Linda Salmon, Summer 1981, Mesa, Arizona

Mae Wills, interview conducted by Linda Salmon, Summer 1981, Globe, Arizona

Exie Zieser, interview conducted by Linda Salmon, Summer 1981, Phoenix, Arizona

SELECTED BIBLIOGRAPHY

Armitage, Susan, and Elizabeth Jameson, eds. *The Women's West*. Norman, Okla.: University of Oklahoma Press, 1987.

Aulette, Judy, and Trudy Mills. "Something Old, Something New: Auxiliary Work in the 1983–1986 Copper Strike." *Feminist Studies* 14, no. 2 (Summer 1988), 251–68.

Bataille, Gretchen M., and Kathleen Mullen Sands. *American Indian Women: Telling Their Lives*. Lincoln, Nebr.: University of Nebraska Press, 1984.

Blair, Karen J. *The Clubwoman as Feminist: True Womanhood Redefined, 1868–1914*. New York: Holmes and Meier Publishers, Inc., 1980.

Bush, Corky, Katherine Jensen, and Mary Aickin Rothschild. "Three Generations of an Oral History-Readers Theater Project." *Frontiers: A Journal of Women's Studies*, vol. 7, no. 1 (1983), 80–90.

Bush, Corlann Gee. "The Way We Weren't: Images of Women and Men in Cowboy Art." In Susan Armitage and Elizabeth Jameson, eds., *The Women's West*. Norman, Okla.: University of Oklahoma Press, 1987, 19–33.

Bushman, Claudia, ed. *Mormon Sisters: Women in Early Utah*. Cambridge, Mass.: Emmeline Press Ltd., 1976.

Catt, Carrie Chapman, and Nettie Rogers Shuler. *Woman Suffrage and Politics: The Inside Story of the Suffrage Movement*. Seattle, Wash.: University of Washington Press, 1970.

Chafe, William H. *The American Woman: Her Changing Social, Economic and Political Roles, 1920–1970*. New York: Oxford University Press, 1972.

Crowe, Rosalie, and Diane Tod, eds. *Arizona Women's Hall of Fame*. Phoenix: Arizona Historical Society, 1986.

de Gennera, Nat, ed., *Arizona Statistical Abstract, 1979 Edition*. Tucson, Ariz.: Division of Economic and Business Research. The University of Arizona, 1980.

D'Emilio, John, and Estelle B. Freedman. *Intimate Matters: A History of Sexuality in America*. New York: Harper and Row, 1988.

Deutsch, Sarah. *No Separate Refuge: Culture, Class and Gender on an Anglo-Hispanic Frontier in the American Southwest, 1880–1940*. New York: Oxford University Press, 1987.

Deutsch, Sarah. "Women and Intercultural Relations: The Case of Hispanic New Mexico and Colorado." *Signs* 12, no.4 (Summer 1987),
719–39.

Dye, Nancy Schrom. "History of Childbirth in America." *Signs* 6, no.
1 (Autumn, 1980), 97–108.

Faragher, John Mack. *Women and Men on the Overland Trail*. New Haven,
Conn.: Yale University Press, 1979.

Faulk, Odie. *Arizona: A Short History*. Norman, Okla.: University of
Oklahoma Press, 1988.

Faunce, Hilda. *Desert Wife*. Lincoln, Nebr.: University of Nebraska
Press, 1981.

Fischer, Christiane. "A Profile of Women in Arizona in Frontier Days."
Journal of the West 16, no. 3 (July 1977), 42–53.

———. *Let Them Speak for Themselves: Women in the American West,
1849–1900*. Hamden, Conn.: Archon Books, 1977.

Goldman, Marion S. *Gold Diggers and Silver Miners: Prostitution and Social Life on the Comstock Lode*. Ann Arbor, Mich.: University of Mich-
igan Press, 1981.

Gluck, Sherna Berger, and Daphne Patai. *Women's Words: The Feminist
Practice of Oral History*. New York: Routledge, 1991.

Grimes, Alan P. *The Puritan Ethic and Woman Suffrage*. New York: Oxford University Press, 1967.

Griswold, Robert. "Apart But Not Adrift: Wives, Divorce, and Independence in California, 1850–1890." *Pacific Historical Review* 49 (May
1980), 265–83.

Hampsten, Elizabeth. *Read This Only to Yourself: The Private Writings of
Midwestern Women, 1880–1910*. Bloomington, Ind.: Indiana University Press, 1982.

Jameson, Elizabeth. "Toward a Multicultural History of Women in the
Western United States." *Signs* 13, no. 4 (Summer 1988), 761–91.

Jeffrey, Julie Roy. *Frontier Women: The Trans-Mississippi West, 1840–1880*.
New York: Hill and Wang, 1979.

Jensen, Joan M., and Darlis A. Miller. "The Gentle Tamers Revisited:
New Approaches to the History of Women in the American West."
Pacific Historical Review, 49 (May 1980), 173–213.

———. *New Mexico Women: Intercultural Perspectives*. Albuquerque,
N.M.: University of New Mexico Press, 1986.

Johnson, Susan. "Women's Households and Relationships in the Mining
West: Central Arizona, 1863–1873." Unpublished Master's Thesis.
Arizona State University, 1984.

Kelly, Rita Mae, ed. *Women and the Arizona Political Process.* Lanham, Md.: University Press of America, Inc., 1988.

Kessler-Harris, Alice. *Out to Work: A History of Wage-Earning Women in the United States.* New York: Oxford University Press, 1982.

Kolodny, Annette. *The Land Before Her: Fantasy and Experience of the American Frontiers, 1630–1860.* Chapel Hill, N.C.: University of North Carolina Press, 1984.

Kraditor, Aileen. *The Ideas of the Woman Suffrage Movement, 1890–1920.* New York: W. W. Norton and Co., 1981.

Larson, T. A. "Woman Suffrage in Western America." *Utah Historical Quarterly,* 28 (1970), 7–19.

Leavitt, Judith Walzer. *Brought to Bed: Childbearing in America, 1790–1950.* New York: Oxford University Press, 1986.

Luckingham, Bradford. *Phoenix: The History of a Southwestern Metropolis.* Tucson, Ariz.: University of Arizona Press, 1989.

———. "Urban Development in Arizona: The Rise of Phoenix." *Journal of Arizona History* 22 (Summer 1981), 197–234.

———. *The Urban Southwest: A Profile History of Albuquerque, El Paso, Phoenix and Tucson.* El Paso, Tex.: Texas Western Press, University of Texas, El Paso, 1982.

Luchetti, Cathy, and Carol Olwell. *Women of the West.* St. George, Utah: Antelope Island Press, 1982.

Matsumoto, Valerie. " 'Shikata Ga Nai': Japanese American Women in Central Arizona, 1910–1978." Unpublished Honor's Thesis. Arizona State University, 1978.

Melcher, Mary. "The Phoenix Civil Rights Movement: Black and White Collaboration, 1950–1970." Unpublished Paper, 1990.

———. "Madge Copeland and Placida Garcia Smith: Community Organizers, Phoenix, Arizona, 1930–1960." Unpublished Paper.

———. " 'Women's Matters': Prenatal Care, Birth Control and Childbirth in Rural Montana, 1910–1940." Unpublished Paper Presented at the "Twentieth Century Western Women's History Research Conference," Arizona State University, October 20, 1989.

Mitchell, Olive Kimball B. *Life is a Fulfilling . . . The Story of a Mormon Pioneer Woman—Sarah Diantha Gardner Curtis and Her Part in the Colonization of the San Pedro Valley in Southern Arizona, the Homeland of the Powerful, Antagonistic Apache.* Provo, Utah: Brigham Young University Press, 1967.

Moynihan, Ruth B., Susan Armitage, and Christiane Fischer Dichamp.

So Much to Be Done: Women Settlers on the Mining and Ranching Frontier. Lincoln, Nebr.: University of Nebraska Press, 1990.

Myres, Sandra L. *Westering Women and the Frontier Experience, 1800–1915.* Albuquerque, N.M.: University of New Mexico Press, 1982.

Noble, Marguerite. *Filaree: A Novel of American Life.* New York: Random House, 1979.

Norwood, Vera, and Janice Monk, eds. *The Desert Is No Lady: Southwestern Landscapes in Women's Writing and Art.* New Haven, Conn.: Yale University Press, 1987.

Riley, Glenda. *Women and Indians on the Frontier, 1825–1915.* Albuquerque, N.M.: University of New Mexico Press, 1984.

Rothschild, Mary Aickin, and Pamela Claire Hronek, "A History of Arizona Women's Politics." In Rita Mae Kelly, ed., *Women and the Arizona Political Process.* Lanham, Md.: University Press of America, 1988, 5–20.

Schlissel, Lillian. *Women's Diaries of the Westward Journey.* New York: Schocken Books, 1982.

Schlissel, Lillian, Byrd Gibbens, and Elizabeth Hampsten. *Far from Home: Families of the Westward Journey.* New York: Schocken Books, 1989.

Schlissel, Lillian, Vicki L. Ruiz, and Janice Monk, eds. *Western Women: Their Land, Their Lives.* Albuquerque, N.M.: University of New Mexico Press, 1988.

Scholten, Catherine M. "On the Importance of the Obstetric Art: Changing Customs of Childbirth in America." *William and Mary Quarterly* 34 (July 1971), 426–46.

Snapp, Meredith. "Defeat the Democrats: The Arizona Campaigns of the Congressional Union for Woman Suffrage." Unpublished Master's Thesis. Arizona State University, 1976.

———. "Defeat the Democrats: Union for Woman Suffrage in Arizona, 1914–1916." *Journal of the West* 14 (October 1975), 131–39.

Stratton, Joanna L. *Pioneer Women: Voices from the Kansas Frontier.* New York: Simon and Schuster, 1981.

Summerhayes, Martha. *Vanished Arizona: Recollections of the Army Life of a New England Woman.* Lincoln, Neb.: University of Nebraska Press, 1979.

Trimble, Marshall. *Arizona: A Calvalcade of History.* Tucson, Ariz.: Treasure Chest Publications, 1989.

U.S. Department of Commerce, Bureau of the Census. *Characteristics of the Population, 1970 Census of Population.* Arizona. Washington, D.C.: Government Printing Office, 1973.

U. S. Department of Commerce, Bureau of the Census. *Fifteenth Census of the United States: 1930, Population.* Washington, D.C.: Government Printing Office, 1932.

U. S. Department of Commerce, Bureau of the Census. *Fourteenth Census of the United States: 1920, Population.* Washington, D.C.: Government Printing Office, 1922.

Walker, Henry P., and Don Bufkin. *Historical Atlas of Arizona.* Norman, Okla.: University of Oklahoma, 1989.

Welter, Barbara. "The Cult of True Womanhood." *American Quarterly* 18 (Summer 1966), 131–75.

INDEX

✦

ABOUT THE AUTHORS

MARY LOGAN ROTHSCHILD is an associate professor of history at Arizona State University. Her field is twentieth-century women's history, and she is especially interested in women's daily lives and how they fashion their communities. She is currently writing a book on Girl Scouting as a social movement, which will focus on the social construction of girlhood and adolescence in America. With her first study, *A Case of Black and White: Northern Volunteers and the Southern Freedom Summers, 1964–1965*, she began to work in the field of oral history. *Doing What the Day Brought* comes out of her desire to continue doing oral history, her definition of herself as a fourth generation western woman and her passion to see women portrayed accurately as real contributors to the development of the West.

PAMELA CLAIRE HRONEK is an associate professor of history at Arkansas State University in Jonesboro, Arkansas. She teaches courses on women's history, twentieth century history, women in the Trans-Mississippi West, and the history of American education. Hronek has written on the history of women's education in the United States—particularly in the West—and on methods of teaching history in the public schools. She is currently working on a book on women and normal school education.